Indian Cookbook For Beginners

Prepare Over 100 Tasty, Traditional And Innovative Indian Recipes To Spice Up Your Meals With This Comprehensive Cookbook (2022 Edition)

Celia Adkins

INTRODUCTION

India, the vast landmass of South Asia, is home to one of the world's greatest and most powerful civilizations. We're all well aware of the Indians' penchant for fine cuisine. We are always eager to talk about cooking, eating, and experimenting with new recipes. Certainly, every single household in India has its own recipe that has been passed down from generation to generation.

But how much do we know about Indian cuisine's history? As a result, the voyage of Indian food heritage will be described in this issue.

Throughout its more than 4,000-year history, India has attracted a large number of immigrants from various religious traditions. To comprehend the dynamics of India's native food culture, one must first recognize that the country is far from culturally homogeneous. A large portion of the food is made up of regional and sectarian dishes. The name "Indian food" was coined, which a native will certainly scoff at because it is akin to saying "North American wine" to a wine specialist. Many regions in India have their own unique cooking methods, flavors, and fresh ingredients. With a population of nearly a billion people, its food diversity is as diverse as its inhabitants.

Muslims and Hindus are the two dominant groups that have had the greatest impact on Indian cuisine's culture and dietary preferences. With each native movement, they established their own dietary customs. There is a prevalent practice of vegetarian Hinduism. In comparison, Muslim culture is the most prevalent in terms of meat cookery. Mughlai cuisine, kababs, nargisi kaftas, biryani, and favorite dishes cooked in the tandoor are some of the many advantages offered by Muslim residents in India. South Indian cuisine is primarily rice-based, with a thin porridge accent known as Rasam. Coconut is a vital ingredient in any Indian cuisine. Dosa and idli are popular vegetarian meals in Hindu culture. In addition, the Portuguese, Persians, and British made significant contributions to Indian cuisine. Tea was introduced to India by the British, and it is now a popular beverage among many Indians.

North, East, South, and West are the four major geographical styles of Indian cookery. The history of North India was influenced by the Mughal Empire, which ruled for 300 years before being replaced by the British in the 18th century. Naan bread, which is baked in a tandoor, is not indigenous to India. It is a daily meal for the Afghani people. Naan is not the bread that Indians eat on a regular basis, but it has been a prevalent misconception about Indian food outside the country for decades.

Specific steamed rice cakes are popular among Southern Indians. Rice is consumed at all meals, and lunch is generally made up of all meal courses, each of which is filled with rice. Vegetarians and nonvegetarians are two types of Hindus. The coconut, the state's culinary emblem, is a common thread across Kerala's Southern Region. The western states of Gujarat, Maharashtra, and Goa all have distinct health experiences. Gujarat is mostly populated by Muslims, Hindus, Parsis, and Jains, each of whom has their own cuisine style. Parsis eat a lot of poultry and seafood. Gujaratis are mostly vegetarians, and Gujarat is considered one of the best places to eat vegetarian food. Maharashtra is a vast state known for its famous metropolis of Mumbai. The states in the east are quite distinct. Bengali cuisine, with fish and rice at its heart, can be described as delicate and subtle. A Bengali lunch begins with a bitter-tasting mixed vegetable dish and ends with a rich, sweet dessert based on milk, for which Bengali is famous. Squash blossoms folded in rice and deep-fried paste or converted into patties are popular in Orissa. Cod and other fish are also included in the diet.

Chicken is rarely eaten here, and fowl plays a small culinary role in general. People in Bihar and Jharkhand eat a lot of vegetables and legumes, but their diet also includes beef, pork, goat, and fowl. Indian food is only linked by its geographical location from East to West, but its taste is clearly limitless.

An Overview of Traditional Indian Dishes

The history of Indian food is the result of the creativity of many societies during times of necessity and succession. Such foods were made for the general public's sake, while others were imported from all over the world. Many of those amazing Indian cuisine stories are now unknown to the general public. Some of the traditional Indian customs are explained below.

Petha predates the Taj Mahal.

Petha in Agra is the best option for consumption. The development of the Taj Mahal during the Mughals is relevant to the invention. When the huge shrine was housed beneath a building, the daily supper of dal and roti bored approximately 20,000 laborers. The Mughal Emperor Shah Jahan then communicated his concern to the master architect, Ustad Isa Effendi, who demanded a response from Pir Naqshbandi Sahib to the Emperor's difficulties. It is said that one day, while praying, the Pir went into a trance and gave Mughal Petha's formula. Petha was then rendered for the staff by around 500 cooks.

Dal Bati was a survival tool during wars.

This is the best meal in Rajasthan. Dal Bati's recipe is a story worth telling. This Rajasthani dish has its origins in the well-known Mewar Chittorgarh Fort. Bati is fried wheat flatbread in oil, a sustenance that the Mewar Rajput monarchs needed to survive in adverse combat conditions. With limited resources and little water available, bati might be grown in Rajasthan's desert plains.

The Mysore Monarchy yielded to the Commons.

It is a well-known sweetmeat in South India. Mysore's history is linked to the early twentieth-century Mysore Palace kitchen. The royal cook at Mysore Palace used to dazzle the King with a variety of meals. One day, he created a new sweet dish out of chickpea flour, oil, and sugar.

When asked what the name of the sauce was, the cook devised the term "Mysore Paka" in a split second. "Paka" is a Kannada term that refers to a sweet concoction.

Khaja is a descendant of both the Mauryan and Gupta empires.

While the cooking art of making Khaja is a source of pride for the people of Orissa, the technique is said to have been adopted from Bihar's central highlands some 2200 years ago. Khaja's ancestors can be traced back to the ancient Indian Gupta empires. Rajgir's Khaja in Bihar is well-known for its swelling, whilst Kakinada's Khaja in Andhra Pradesh is well-known for its dry outside yet tasty inside.

Jalebi's Culture Isn't Always Indian

Jalebi, one of India's most popular sweet desserts, has its origins in West Asia.

The Persian-speaking conquerors brought jalebi to India in the Middle Ages. In the 14th century, this sweetmeat was known as "Kundalika" and "Jalavallika" in India. During Ramadan, the destitute in Iran were given platefuls of jalebi.

Dum Biryani Provided Meals to the Needy in Awadh

According to historical documents, the origins of biryani can be traced back to the provincial capital of Hyderabad during the Nawab dynasty. According to some, biryani was invented during Timur's invasion of India in the early medieval age. While the origins of biryani are debated, Dum Biryani, or Awadh's Biryani, evolved in Lucknow. When food was short, the Nawab of Awadh commanded all the poor people in his domain to cook a supper in large handis (round-shaped metal pots). With limited energy, a significant amount of food was cooked in covered and sealed pans. This cooking technique is known as "dum."

Indian Cuisine and Its Popularity in the United States

Indian cuisine is growing in popularity in the United States. Right now, it's like a very specialized dish. Apart from Chinese cuisine, which is nearly ubiquitous in the US, the food network reveals even more references to Indian cuisine, and Indian ingredients are appearing everywhere in the US. Due to their delicious taste, Indian foods have gained popularity around the world. Several delectable Indian dishes are prepared at various dining establishments across the country. As Indian restaurants have flourished at an unprecedented rate, with tremendous appeal in every imaginable community and in every imaginable corner of the globe, many fans on a global scale have noted the vast array of salads, appetizers, sweets, side dishes, and desserts.

India is the world's largest fruit grocer. India has enormous scientific and engineering capacity, which is rapidly being applied to the production of modern, popular food products in the United States. New items are still in demand, so there is enormous potential for new products, particularly in the United States, where people enjoy eating Indian food. The success of American Indian food has also fueled a trend among Indian enterprises to sell more food to the United States.

Indian cuisine is well-known throughout the world for its aromatic flavors and spices. The numerous Indian restaurants in Washington, DC produce delectable delicacies and serve them to both visitors and residents of the area.

Every location has a distinct culinary art that is unlike any other. These approaches were brought to Western countries and quickly gained widespread popularity among individuals. The unique dish is prepared for special occasions. Many overseas shoppers have been captivated by the spices and various ingredients needed to prepare such cuisines.

It is critical to note that most Indian spices have medicinal properties. Turmeric, ginger, and cardamom are the most commonly utilized herbs due to their therapeutic benefits. This is one of the main reasons why individuals in the United States are eager to consume Indian food, stating that the spices used have medical powers and would not harm their bodies in any manner. This book will teach you everything you need to know about Indian cuisine, the spices that are commonly used in it, and 100 recipes.

CHAPTER 1: UNDERSTANDING THE FUNDANENTALS OF INDIAN CUISINE

Indian cuisine includes a variety of current and traditional Indian subcontinent cuisines. These dishes range significantly due to the variation of geography, climate, history, ethnic groups, and vocations, and use herbs, vegetables, and fruits accessible locally. Furthermore, Indian food is strongly linked to religion, particularly Hinduism, as well as social decisions and rituals.

In a Nutshell: Indian Regional Foods

It is common for Indian restaurants to present dishes as part of a standardized, nationalized cuisine. India's food is as regionally distinct and diversified as its people. These dishes are heavily influenced by India's history, trade links, and cultural and religious traditions. A little background on the similarities and differences between India's regional cuisines will turn your next Indian meal into an entertaining and profoundly satisfying experience.

While Indian food is largely regionally distinct, there are certain common threads that link the various cooking practices. Sauces, which are sauce-like sauces or soup-like meat, potato, or cheese dishes, are heavily used in Indian cuisine across the country. On the other hand, the distinctive spice mixes, fluidity amounts, and ingredients, on the other hand, are determined by regional preference. In general, Indian cuisine is heavily reliant on agriculture, with the Southern Indian regions relying more heavily on rice than other regions. Both regional foods rely on legumes, sometimes known as "pulses." Indian cuisine can employ a broader variety of peas than any other menu item: Red lentils, black gram, peas or yellow gram, black gram, and green gram are used whole, split, or processed in flour in a variety of Indian recipes. Tartness may be added to non-egg meals, legumes can be added to vegan diets, and nutrition can be added to vegetarian diets.

The extensive use of spices is undoubtedly the most distinctive element of Indian cuisine. Indian spice blends often contain up to five distinct spices, with ten or more added on occasion. Garam masala is a popular spice blend that includes cardamom, cinnamon, and clove, with the precise spices varying by region and personal recipe.

Indicated Observations: Commerce and Invasion

The cultural impact of trade is visible in Indian cuisine, with distinct locales and cuisines bearing the mark of international influence. In addition, Arab and Canadian traders coveted India's spices; in exchange, India received various items that significantly altered its culinary legacy. Portuguese traders brought in new world items like onions, peppers, and chillies, which were heavily incorporated into Indian recipes. Arab merchants transported coffee.

The nature of India's delicacies has also been profoundly influenced by its occupancy times. Mughal invaders infused Persian flavors and practices into Indian culinary culture between the early 1500s and the late 1600s. The influence is visible in the use of cheese and milk in sauces, as well as the usage of meat and nuts in salads, particularly in green salads.

The British rule in India introduced the country to soup and tea, but had no effect on its food. The imperial assimilation of native food into British society, on the other hand, has had a profound influence on Indian food translation abroad. Tikka Masala, a savory sauce found in many Indian cuisines, is an Anglo-Indian creation that is popularly regarded as "Britain's true national dish." Even European perceptions of Indian "curry"—the name refers to a variety of garlicky and stew-like dishes—are derived from British understanding of Indian cuisine.

India has a large community.

India's population is very diverse, with ethnic and religious differences strongly influencing cultural traditions. Ayurvedic traditions exerted an influence on Indian cuisine in particular, attempting to mandate spice combinations and cooking procedures while emphasizing the balance of the brain, body, and spirit. According to religious and cultural traits, this hypothesis has a popular influence in Indian cuisine.

Vegetarianism is practiced by almost one-third of India's population as a result of Hindu, Jain, or Buddhist ideals. As a result, a substantial chunk of Indian cuisine in the United States is devoid of meat. Furthermore, religious traditions affect the dietary limitations that comprise India's cuisine: Hindus refrain from eating meat because livestock is sacred in their religion, whereas Muslims feel pork is filthy and will never consume it. Depending on the predominant religious beliefs in a specific location, the cuisine in that area may prohibit those components in order to adhere to religious regulations.

Northern Indian Cuisine.

Northern Indian food, which is possibly the most common cuisine encountered outside of India, has a strong Mughal influence. It is marked by high dairy consumption: milk, paneer (a mild Indian cheese), butter, and yoghurt are all popular ingredients in northern recipes. Samosas, and sometimes beef, are a popular northern delicacy. Tandoors, or clay ovens, are common in the North, imparting a distinct barbeque flavor to dishes such as naan. A large variety of northern dishes can be found in Indian restaurants on a daily basis. Dal or Paneer Makhani is a popular vegetarian dish that consists of dal or paneer sautéed in a creamy tomato sauce with oignons, mango dust, and curry powder. Another Northern Indian favorite, Korma, is a creamy dish made with coconut milk or yoghurt, cumin, cilantro, and a few cashews or walnuts. It goes well with a variety of meats, most notably poultry or lamb, but also beef and a vegan dish with paneer.

West Indian Food

Western regional cuisine is distinguished by the region's political and cultural characteristics. Maharashtra's coastal region is well-known for its milk-dominated seafood and coconut cuisine. Gujarati cuisine is primarily vegetarian, and most dishes have an innate sweetness as a result of strong influences. Because of the dry climate, this region is well known for its chutneys, which are traditional Indian condiments that blend fried, fresh, or marinated fruits and vegetables with sweet, sour, or spicy flavors. Goa served as a major port and commercial colony for Portugal, resulting in a unique blend of Indian and Portuguese cuisine. Beef and pork are used more frequently in Goa cuisine than in other Indian cuisines. Vinegar is another distinguishing feature of Goan cuisine. Because of its coastal location, coconut milk, coconut powder, and fish are common ingredients in Goan cuisine.

Indian cuisine from the east

Eastern regional cuisine is well-known for its desserts. These treats are not only popular in other Indian states, but they are also available in restaurants. Their delicate sweetness makes an excellent meal conclusion. Rasgulla is a popular sweet dessert made of semolina balls and cheese curd cooked in light sugar syrup. Eastern cuisines like mustard seeds and mustard oil, which add a pleasant aroma to the food. Rice and fish are also popular in Eastern cuisine. Eastern dishes are generally more spicy than meals from other countries.

Indian Southern Cuisine:

Southern Indian food is not commonly found on restaurant menus and is distinct from other locations. Their "curries" vary widely in appearance and are usually categorised according to whether they are drier or prefer a more stew-like or soupy appearance. Poriyals are dry curries comprised of vegetables and seasonings, served as a side dish to rice.

Sambars are essentially tamarind-flavored pea and vegetable soups that are soupier than curries from many other nations but smoother than rasams. Rasams are similar to soups in terms of quality and are made primarily with tomatoes, tamarind, and a variety of spices. Kootus is more like other areas' curries, but instead of being fluffy like the North's dairy-based curries, it gets its robustness from drained lentils.

Southern Indian cuisine is well-known for its beautiful fried or griddle-cooked sweets, as well as curry-style entrees. Dosas are a type of crepe.

They are typically filled with vegetable curries, sauces, or seasonings.

Idli is a fried treat similar to savory doughnuts served with sambar and rasam. Apart from establishments directly serving Southern Indian cuisine, the only South Indian item often found at Indian restaurants is pappadams, fried crispy rice cookies commonly flavored with black peppercorns.

1.2 Characteristics of Indian Food

Indian cuisine has crossed all territorial boundaries and entered international territory. Today, everyone appears to recognize and enjoy Tandoori chicken, Pav Bhaji, and Kesar kulfi. Foodies all over the world are huge lovers of both vegetarian and non-vegetarian Indian dishes.

The Existing Pattern

Customers are increasingly visiting the world's most notable Indian restaurants and indulging in their famed Indian culinary delights. Indian cuisine is rapidly expanding up the food chain.Tandoori is a popular dish all around the world. North Indian cuisine is incredibly tasty. Tandoori appetizers such as Tandoori Chicken, Reshmi Kebabs, and much more will leave you wanting more.

Surprising Wealth

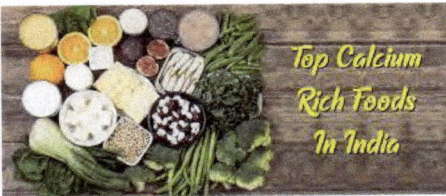

Due to its outstanding variety, Indian food has grown in popularity over the years. There is something for every taste bud in Indian food. Some people are fascinated by South Indian delicacies; others are fascinated by Punjabi delicacies; still others are obsessed with Rajasthani or Goa food, Parsi food, or mouth-watering Bengali meals. By introducing a few fusion varieties, Indian street cuisine has been given new life.

The Unstoppable Ratio of Food

Most Indian cuisines are cooked in such a way that the nutritious content of all goods is kept and not harmed as a result of the cooking procedure. A variety of spices contribute to the authentic experience and flavors of Indian cuisine. These spices are beneficial to the skin. It sells pickles and greens in several parts of India. Their flavors are unique to the location, but they might pique your interest.

1.3 The Importance and Benefits of Indian Foods in Your Diet

Taking these factors into account, we have compiled a list of essential Indian foods that should be included in everyone's diet. Remember, if you are suffering from any medical problem, please see your doctor about what you may and may not take from this chart.

Fruits

Many traditional Indian fruits are ideal for you. They include a wide range of critical vitamins and minerals that are vital to our health. Strawberries, bananas, pomegranates, pineapples, and other seasonal and annual fruits can be consumed on a daily basis. People with such health issues should avoid particular fruits, but for the average citizen, these are perfect healthy foods to supplement the fried chip bag. Fruits have the following health benefits:

Fruits contain a variety of essential elements that are underutilized, such as calcium, dietary fiber, and vitamin C.

Most fruits are typically low in sugar, salt, and energy. However, as you consume fruit, your energy production increases quickly; this is one of the fruit's key benefits that we can include in our hectic schedules.

The fiber component in the fruit not only has a wonderful soothing impact, but it also helps you feel full when introducing bulk protein into your diet.

Chilies

New chilies, more than any other vegetable, are exceptionally high in vitamin C. You've come to the right place if you like spicy food. There are lots of "less hard" chilies available for individuals who prefer milder spicy dishes that can provide the same benefits without the burning sensation. Chilies, too, boost the metabolism. Health Benefits of Chilies:

Chili contains up to 7 times as much vitamin C as orange, which has a variety of health benefits including fighting sinus inflammation, increasing metabolism, relieving headaches, and relieving heart, joint, and nerve pain.

Chili has long been used to reduce bio-contamination in food and is frequently thought to be a viable weight loss metabolic accelerator.

It can also help in the treatment of leukemia and lung cancer.

Beans

They're an excellent source of protein, calcium, magnesium, and folic acid. They are also adaptable, allowing you to cook a variety of Indian meals.

They also accompany different communities' cuisines, ranging from Asian to American.

Beans' Advantages:

Beans are "heart-friendly" because they include soluble fiber, which lowers cholesterol levels. The majority of beans have 2 to 3% fat and no cholesterol unless cooked or mixed with other foods.

Beans are high in fiber, which helps to prevent acid reflux and promotes regularity. Consumption of beans on a daily basis lowers the risk of cardiovascular disease.

Garlic

BENEFITS OF GARLIC
- Regulates blood pressure and sugar
- Strengthens immune system
- Prevents heart disease
- Detoxification
- Anti-inflammatory
- Prevents and treats cold
- Improves bone health
- Lowers cholesterol
- Antioxidants
- Anti-cancer

Garlic is not only delicious, but it is also well-known for its multiple therapeutic properties. It's an important natural source of antibacterial agents. Garlic has the following nutritional benefits:

Garlic produces a labeled allicin molecule that has powerful therapeutic properties.

Because of allicin's antioxidant properties, frequent consumption of garlic (raw or cooked) tends to lower total cholesterol.

Garlic's energizing characteristics protect the body from free radicals and decrease collagen depletion, which leads to loss of conductivity in aging skin.

Spices

Since ancient times, Indian spices have gained international acclaim. Aside from their excellent flavor and taste, certain spices are also good for you. Haldi, also known as turmeric, has calming properties, aids in cholesterol reduction, and prevents blood clots, which can lead to heart attacks.

Cardamom boosts metabolism, and the spices in garam masala provide a variety of nutrients that aid in digestion. Spices have the following nutritional benefits:

Many herbs and spices contain more antioxidants to fight disease than veggies and fruits.

Cinnamon has anti-diabetic properties and lowers blood sugar levels.

Turmeric contains curcumin, a substance with potent antioxidant properties.

Ginger has anti-inflammatory properties and may help with nausea.

Paneer

It is a staple of the vegetarian diet, although it is also popular among nonvegetarians. Paneer is a versatile ingredient that may be used in a variety of cuisines. You can also avoid the muscle-building kind generated by whole milk. Homemade breadcrumbs prepared from milk have far fewer fatty acids and cholesterol, making them far healthier. However, the high amino and calcium concentrations can be maintained. paneer benefits:

Paneer is a high source of protein, especially for vegetarian diets that do not obtain their meat intake.

Because paneer is made of protein, it slowly absorbs energy into the bloodstream, preventing a surge in blood sugar levels.

'Aside from being high in protein, paneer is an excellent source of linoleic acid—a fatty acid that aids in weight loss by stimulating the body's fat-burning mechanism.

It avoids a variety of health problems, including osteoporosis, knee pain, and dental concerns such as tooth decay and gum disease.

Rice and flour.

White rice is the most consumed grain in India. Brown rice, on the other hand, contains more protein and is therefore a safer alternative. The use of whole wheat flour is becoming more widespread. You should recommend doing the same for other wheat products, such as bread.

Rice and flour have the following health benefits:

Our bodies require insoluble fibers to help them get rid of waste, so if constipation is an issue, rice and flour will help, as will nuts, beans, and vegetables like cabbage, all of which provide the majority of the fiber.

Rice and flour are high in protein and have a high level of B vitamins.

'Dietary fiber is an essential component of any diet. Rice provides dietary fiber and aids in the passage of waste items through the digestive tract.

Pulses

The Indian diet is extremely grain-rich. Rice and pasta are the most common examples, but pulses are also an important element of our diet. Fortunately, there are so many different types of pulses available that variety can always be maintained in your diet. Pulses are high in fiber as well as vitamins A, B, C, and E. They, too, produce minerals like calcium and iron. They are, by far, the most important source of nourishment in a vegetarian diet.

Pulse Health Benefits:

Including more pulses in your diet can lower your risk of heart disease.

Pulses are the item with the most sugar. The sugar content of the diet is listed in terms of how it affects blood sugar. Pulses are frequently used to make protein a safe and inexpensive source.

Green, leafy vegetables

Green-leaved veggies are already common in the Indian diet. They can, however, be put to better use. Spinach can be found throughout the region all year round. Cabbage is also accessible in a variety of locations throughout the year. Furthermore, depending on where you live in the world, hundreds of different types of leafy greens are ready to be included in your diet.

The health benefits of leafy vegetables are as follows:

Mustard and kale greens can lower cholesterol.

Leafy greens help to retain strong vision, lower the likelihood of cataracts, and improve the clarity with which you can see.

They help to fuel the body and generate electricity, and they have a mildly acidic flavor, which reflects their high calcium content.

Continue with the eggs.

Although they are not always suitable for vegetarian diets, they are high in protein. Even if you avoid eating the entire egg, the egg white will assist your body in receiving the vital vitamins and nutrients. Almost any dish can benefit from the addition of eggs. Eggs provide the following health benefits:

Eggs are an excellent source of free, high-quality protein.

Feeding tiny children one egg each day for six months, combined with a reduced sugar-sweetened diet, can help them achieve a healthy height.

Eggs are high in cholesterol but have no harmful effects on cholesterol levels in the body.

Eggs are high in nutrients that help protect the heart.

1.4 The Health Benefits of Eating Indian Food

The inclusion of spices such as onion, turmeric, ginger, and garlic in the dish leads to a number of health benefits, such as lower cholesterol, a lower risk of cancer, and improved renal function. While we all know that Indian food has many health benefits, including spices and veggies, you may be surprised to learn that Indian food is not always safe. The majority of Indian cuisine is vegetarian. According to research, eating a plant-based diet has a number of advantages. Some of these benefits are as follows:

A Vegetarian Diet That Is Healthy

The Indian cuisine is ideal for nutritional recipes since they use a wide variety of vegetables, lentils, and grains. The rice blend that allows you to acquire a complete protein. Because Indians consume a wide range of foods on a daily basis, all of the minerals and vitamins present in various plants are more likely to be absorbed.

The veggies in these recipes provide a variety of minerals and antioxidants that are beneficial to one's health, liver, and brain. Sulfur compounds found in garlic, cauliflower, and cabbage, for example, aid in the detoxification of the body from mycotoxins and harmful poisons.

Anti-Inflammatory Action

Turmeric and other spices have anti-inflammatory qualities and can help prevent a variety of chronic diseases. They frequently aid in the relief of inflammation.

Other spices help to reduce inflammation, boost metabolism, control weight, and detoxify the body. Cinnamon is frequently used to regulate blood sugar levels. If you enjoy hot and spicy Indian food, the chile is your best friend, not only for your taste buds but also for your overall health.Chilies include vitamin C and vitamin A.

Increased fiber concentrations

Chickpeas, green vegetables, corn, grains, lentils, green beans, and other high-fiber foods include chickpeas, green vegetables, corn, grains, lentils, and green beans. Soluble fibers from peas and beans produce a gel-like material when immersed in water. It has an important role in lowering cholesterol and managing blood sugar levels. Insoluble dietary fiber promotes intestinal regularity and prevents indigestion.

Ghee Wellness Centers

In actuality, ghee is healthy, and when used carefully and in moderation, it has healing properties. Pure cow ghee is an important ingredient in Indian and Ayurvedic medicinal cuisine. Ghee will be used as a substitute for butter, palm oil, and hydrolyzed fat on the market. The reason for this is that ghee's chemical composition is more durable than olive oil's, and it does not burn or go rancid soon. The worry for many vegetable oils on the market is that their molecular structures begin to break down during the heating process. They quickly oxidize and cause a slew of problems in the body by increasing the number of free radicals. And you are well aware of the dangers of saturated fat. On the other hand, clarified butter or ghee protects against pollutants and provides essential fatty acids for hormone production in the body. According to Ayurveda, ghee reduces inflammation, improves nutrition, and boosts metabolism.

1.5 What distinguishes home-cooked Indian food from restaurant food?

South Asian cuisine is salty, greasy, filling, and wonderfully delectable. Indian cuisine is an important part of American-Asian life, whether in the comfort of their own homes or in a neighborhood restaurant. Eating out, on the other hand, was not a common activity among previous generations of South Asian immigrants to the United States.

Many considered it an unneeded privilege, distrusting the recipes or culinary styles of "outside" cuisine, claiming it was tailored for the English taste and defining it as an exclusive practice. It was customary to cook at home, and only on rare occasions would the US-Asian family dine out. Many extended families resided in the same home for up to three families, and dining out was not even an option.

Today, young Asians in the United States are dining out more, bringing their families out for dinner, ordering take-out, and not preparing as much at home as they used to. Dining out for Asian Americans is thus a matter of preference and culture, and is not hampered by generational differences.

What could be better? Is it better to eat at home or go out?

Many Asians in the United States enjoy home-cooked meals because they believe they are unique due to the raw vegetables and the opportunity to bake whatever you want in your own oven. Others claim that going out to eat makes the night more enjoyable, convivial, and relaxing. Although each has advantages and disadvantages, Asians in the United States enjoy a hot curry and prefer it when there is a variety to select from. This is where restaurant cuisine comes in handy, since it provides a variety of dishes for everyone who wants to eat them. So, if you're with your friends, you may choose from a menu and eat whatever you want, but if you're at home, let's just agree that it's easier to eat everything.

Food, on the other hand, may always be roasted at restaurants to accommodate the multitude rather than the individual. For example, Chicken Tikka Masala, for example, is a popular restaurant dish that is likely unnamed in an Asian home when prepared. At home, personalized ingredients are used to produce a cuisine based on family or already acquired recipes. Unique herbs, like achaar, or yoghurt, are used to create a recipe that is tailored to your tastes.

Asians appreciate the cuisine, but they prefer to consume it as rapidly as possible at our tables. Eating in does not always imply eating on time, because making Asian meals at home takes time and requires the use of established fresh products and recipes. Giving love and attention to your home and cooking always pays off, especially if it's something special for someone!

In restaurants, you get a starter, a main course, and a dessert, but this isn't enough for those of you with a big appetite. Because the segment sizes are fairly restricted, you may feel as if you are not getting your money's worth. A lamb balti bowl, for example, might cost between $6 and $8. If you're cooking at home, this amount may be enough for you and your guests, with larger serving sizes and the option to add extra if necessary. As Britain becomes more urbanized, all Asians are becoming victims of the fast-food industry.

This is due to the stressful lives that we all lead. While most elderly people love a decent home-cooked meal, the younger generation finds it more convenient to eat out.

CHAPTER 2: THE PROPERTIES OF COMMON SPICES IN INDIAN CUISINE

A wide variety of spices are used in Indian cuisine. They are combined and used extensively in many recipes. With a minor difference in cooking style, the same spice flavor can be dramatically transformed. We selected many of India's most commonly used spices in order to discover these great items.

Red Chili Powder

Red chili is made from red chili seeds. It is the strongest component of the chili and is only used in small amounts. This material was brought to India by the Americans and the Portuguese and has since become a key ingredient in Indian cuisine. Chili is also utilized in several southern Indian dishes. The main characteristic of chili is its hotness, which is presumably attributable to the capsaicin content. However, there are varieties that also have a lot of scent and flavor.

Sesame seeds with mustard

Brown mustard seeds are the most often used mustard seeds in Indian cuisine. These seeds can be roasted whole to flavor oil, which can then be used to prepare raw food. This favorite oil can also be used as a dipping sauce. Although the seeds are native to Rome, the closest parallel to their use may be found in Buddha's literature, where he utilizes specific seeds to save the life of a child.

Coriander

Coriander is a member of the parsley family, and its seeds are spherical, ridged, and change color from dark green to vivid orange as they mature.

This spice appears to be acidic and delightful, with a light lemony fragrance. This invisibly colored spice is without a doubt the world's oldest and is widely grown in Rajasthan state.

Cinnamon

Cinnamon is a spice with a sweet flavor and a mellow, woody aroma. It is ideal for use in desserts and cakes. Cinnamon has a variety of uses, including adding spice to cuisine. It also aids in the prevention of leukemia and the reduction of cholesterol. It is mostly grown along the Western Ghats of Kerala and Tamil Nadu.

Asafoetida

This is the hardened resin that emerges from the base of a plant. It has a garlic-like sulphur fragrance in its natural state and is very strong. When cooked in oil, however, the aroma fades and the flavor improves dramatically.

Asafoetida is often added to hot oil before any other component. It is renowned for its truffle-like flavor and roasted garlic aroma, and it is used as a seasoning blend and flavoring component in Indian cuisine. Asafoetida is largely grown in Kashmir and parts of Punjab. It is quite good for its flatulence-busting effects.

Cumin

Cumin is derived from the parsley family and is used to add a smokey taste and a pungent smell to most Indian dishes and vegetables. Cumin seeds are fried in their dry form and then boiled before use. When cooking Indian dishes, it is usually the first spice to be applied. It is frequently roasted dry and reduced to dust before being used in meals like pancakes and heavy cream. It is also used to flavor meat, stuffed onions, and a variety of Indian dishes. It is used with caution because it burns swiftly and can become intoxicating.

Saffron

Saffron is the most expensive spice in the world. originally

from Kashmir and derived from the prejudice of crocus

bulbs. Saffron is thought to be more valuable than money.

Its most distinguishing feature is its musky, honey-like

aroma. It is frequently used after soaking in water or milk,

which softens its strong scent and flavor.

Tumeric

Tumeric is another spice from the ginger family. It's

possible that it's the most popular spice in India. Turmeric

has been utilized for hundreds of years in ancient

Ayurvedic medicine, largely as a pigment. The roots of the

Indian-born leafy plant, Curcuma Longa, were used to

create this product. It has an oaky taste and scent, as well as a light smell and flavor. It is found in cooking items as well as skincare products. It has numerous medical applications. It aids in the treatment of skin problems. Its powder has the potential to be utilized to treat open wounds. It also enables the treatment of diabetes.

Cardamom

Due to the amount of physical labor required, it is the world's third most expensive spice. The green cardamom has a moderate and gentle eucalyptus color, whereas the black cardamom is gritty, smoky, and largely utilized for its seeds. Cardamom is most commonly used to enhance the flavor of tea and pudding. It is used to add a rich flavor and aroma to most Indian and other sweet cuisines. It is widely used in the pharmaceutical business. It protects against bad breath and gastrointestinal problems. Patients with diabetes should consume whole, chewed cardamom.

India's Bay Leaf

Despite the fact that both are members of the Lauraceae family, Indian Bay Leaf is significantly distinct from European Bay Leaf. They are the leaves of a cinnamon tree parent, and they are distinguished by the white streaks that run through the root. They are quite light yet have a strong spice flavor.

It is found in northern India, the Himalayan foothills, and Nepal. Sikkim State is India's largest producer, but it is often made from raw or wild plants. It is an essential component of Mughal cuisine and may be found in famous dishes such as Korma and biryani.

Ginger

Ginger is one of India's most valued crops, growing at a rate of around 1,000 tonnes per year. The majority of the time, fresh ginger is used. Dry ginger is only utilized in a few Indian states, including Goa and Kashmir.

There are two primary ginger kinds, named for the port from which they were transported: "Cochin" in Kerala's south and "Calicut" in Kerala's north.

Both are highly fragrant, with approximately 4% essential oil content and minimal fibre content. It is thought to be superior to ginger grown in many other countries due to its gentler and more subtle flavor. In Indian cooking, dried ginger is not as frequent as fresh ginger.

Curry Leaves

Curry leaves, which have nothing to do with spices, are the leaves of a bush in the Rutaceae family native to India and Sri Lanka. This vegetation is both fragrant and welcoming.

The curry tree is currently grown in many sections of India, but it is more common in the south. Because it is simple to cultivate, many households have a plant in their greenhouse. In the north, the leaves are frequently used (for example, combined with potato and pea samosa stuffing). They are used in meat and poultry sauces.

Kalonji/Nigella

This plant's black triangle seeds, often known as black cumin, have a moderate and somewhat bitter taste, with earthy tones and an onion-like pungent flavor. India is the world's largest supplier of kalonji. Egypt and Morocco are the other two producers.

These seeds are also powerful antioxidants and have been linked to a variety of medical effects, including relief from asthma, fever, pneumonia, and other autumn disorders.

Ajowan

Ajowan is another seed spice from the Umbelliferae family. It has a slight bitter, earthy flavor and a scent similar to but stronger than thyme. Cooking (particularly baking) smooths the tendency to affect Ajowan, resulting in a somewhat unusual nutty flavor. Rajasthan is India's major ajowan producer, accounting for 90 percent of total output. In Indian cuisine, it is sometimes used for savory snacks and baked items, and it lends a savory flavor to many vegetable dishes. Its medicinal qualities range from aiding digestion to healing colds and removing bloating.

Mustard (Dark Brown)

It is one of the few seasonings that is as popular in the countries that consume the most flavor, such as Indonesia and India. In Europe and America, mustard seeds are nearly entirely used to make the sauce of the same name, which is derived from a Roman blend of mustard seeds with a particular sourness.

There are three varieties of mustard: pale, brown, and black. The light one is gentler, while the other two are more pungent. It is also included in the traditional spice blend of the North East. In this location, there is an Indian variety of mustard sauce made by soaking mustard seeds for a few days.

Mustard seeds only produce pungency when ground or compressed and mixed with a sour fluid and stabilized with an acidic fluid.

Fenugreek

Fenugreek is a legume family herb. Its plants are utilized fresh, dried, and as seeds. Methi is a Hindi word. It has a strange and sour flavor (toasting the seeds reduces the harshness), and its use in the kitchen is as popular as therapeutic therapy. The seeds are primarily used as a spice in India and Turkey, but India is the primary supplier and purchaser.

It is a necessary ingredient in the preparation of curry. It is used to enhance the flavor of vegetables such as pumpkin in Punjab and is used to make dosa in Southern India. Batter-dosas are delicious Indian rice and dal pancakes (split lentils). It is also used in the Bengali five-spice blend.

According to conventional medicine, it enhances absorption and reduces sugar levels. It is frequently used to treat colitis and is advised for breastfeeding moms since it contains a substance that increases milk supply.

Clove

This delectable spice is the crisp, unnamed blossom of a Myrtle family vine native to the Moluccas island chain. Only until the end of the XVIII century did clove production reach beyond the Moluccas, and supremacy was established. Clove is still grown today, primarily in Indonesia and Tanzania. Although manufacturing in South India began in 1800, most cloves consumed today are imported from Sri Lanka. Clove is only used in blends and masala in Indian cooking. It has a strong smell and flavor. It is also utilized in a variety of rice cuisines.

Cloves contain the highest proportion of volatile oil when compared to other spices, and a small amount goes a long way. Clove is also the seasoning with the highest antioxidant capacity.

The spice of black pepper

Pepper is a spice made from the berries of the Piper nigrum plant. In terms of harvesting and post-harvesting, we have three most common pepper varieties: white pepper, black pepper, and green pepper.

In India, it is native to the southern region of Malabar, and it is currently also grown in Kerala. Black pepper is created by extracting the green drupes only when they are ripe and begin to turn red, and then processing them under controlled conditions.

In the sun or in a furnace, until the humidity content falls below a specified threshold. During the drying process, an oxidation process takes place. In the north, black pepper can be found in a variety of spice blends as well as meat and chicken meals.

Powdered Amchur

This is a sweet and malty spice that is used as a thickening agent and as a dipping sauce. It gives curries, sauces, and chutneys a sour, fruity flavor.

CHAPTER 3:RECIPES FOR INDIAN BREAKFAST

The Indian breakfast recipes can be prepared in a short amount of time and will be beneficial to all of you. This chapter has both Northern India morning meals and Southern India breakfast dishes that can be prepared in a matter of minutes. Take a look at these Indian breakfast and brunch recipes. You can now easily prepare these at home in the mornings by following the recipe.

Vegetable Upma Rava

Time to cook: 20 minutes

2 servings per meal

- ✓ 1 cup rasberry 14 cup peas 1 sliced onion 1 cup diced combined vegetables 3 chopped green chilies 1 tablespoon sliced ginger
- ✓ Just a couple of curry leaves 14 teaspoon mustard seeds 12 teaspoon urad dal Coriander leaves, cut, for marinating Oil 1 teaspoon Season with salt to taste.

Methodology

1) Heat the vegetable oil in a large saucepan over medium-high heat.

2) Stir in the coarsely chopped seeds, red chilies, and ginger. Blend the ingredients thoroughly with a wooden skewer.

3) To properly blend the items, add peas and dal to a pan and tightly flip the pan.

4). Stir fry for a few seconds before adding the curry leaves. Meanwhile, take a cutting board and cut all of the vegetables individually. Put the chopped vegetables in the pan and mix thoroughly.

5) Fill the pan halfway with water and season well with salt. Cover the pan with a lid and cook over medium-high heat.

6) Cook until a thick mixture is formed. Now, for a few minutes, heat a nonstick skillet with 1 tablespoon of oil over medium-high heat and fry the semolina in it.

7) While the vegetables are frying, gradually stir in the cooked semolina.Continue to stir constantly, making sure no clumps form.

8) Cook for 5 minutes on low heat before transferring to a serving bowl. Garnish with cashews and mint leaves if desired.

9) Serve right away.

Sooji Upma with Coconut

Time to cook: 30 minutes

4 person servings

ingredients

2 tablespoons ghee1 cup semolina (sooji)1 teaspoon mustard seedYou can use as much asafetida as you want. 10 organic cashews, split 1 teaspoon Chana dal and urad dal in a bath for at least 10 minutes 1 tablespoon ginger, chopped 1 red onion, thinly sliced 1 green chili, diced 10 curry leaves 4 tbsp fresh green peas 2 1/2 cups of water Use as much salt as you like. 2 teaspoons minced cilantro 1 tablespoon ghee

Methodology

1) Roast the sooji over a medium temperature until moist, stirring often for about 5 minutes. Remove the sooji from the skillet and place it in another dish.

2) You can perform this part of frying sooji ahead of time, saving time for busy mornings.

3) To the same pan, add two teaspoons of oil over medium heat.

4) Add the seeds, hing, cashews, dal ginger, and stir fried for 1 minute, or until they start to change color.

5) Stir in the carrot, green chile, and curry leaves. Cook for a further minute after adding the onions.

6) After a while, add the peas and stir. Heat until the fresh scent of peas emerges.

7) Pour in 3 glasses of water. Then I squeezed lemon zest into it, added cilantro, and thoroughly blended it. If you want to add some sweetness to your Upma, you can use honey or sugar.

8) Bring the water to a boil right away.Start by adding the fried sooji little by little until the water has boiled.

9) Using a dough scraper, mix sooji in one direction after each addition.

10) Place a lid over the pot and reduce the heat to "normal." Allow it to remain that way for a while.

11) Remove the cover and add 2 teaspoon ghee. This is optional, although it is encouraged. Turn off the heat.

12) Warm upma with coconut chutney is served.

Upma Rice with Puffed Upma

Serving size: 1–2 people

Time to cook: 15 minutes.

ingredients

Puffed rice, 3 cups1 teeny-tiny onion 1 teeny-tiny tomato 1 or 2 chilies 12 teaspoon turmeric powder 12 teaspoon mustard seeds 1 dry red chili, sliced Just a couple of curry leaves 2 teaspoons olive oil Season with salt to taste.

Methodologies

1) Chop everything roughly.

2) Heat one tablespoon of oil in a skillet. Fill it with seeds.

3) Toss the fried seeds with the dried red chili and urad dal. Fry till the dal turns brown.

4) Combine all of the chopped ingredients in a large mixing bowl.

5) Season with salt and turmeric to taste.

6) Cover for a minute and set aside to simmer.

7) Take the puffed rice and literally wash it through with running water.Squeeze out the water and quickly return it to the plate.

8) Pour it into a saucepan. fry for a few seconds over high heat.

9) Take it off the heat.

10) Serve the puffed Upma rice right away.

Things to Keep in Mind

✓ Puffed rice should not be washed in water since it becomes soggy.

✓ Wet upma-puffed rice tastes better.

Upma Rice with Tamarind and Rava

Time to cook: 20-30 minutes

6-8 person servings

ingredients

✓ 2 c. Rava rice 1 finely sliced onion 3-4 green chilies, sliced 12 tsp. ginger, coarsely chopped 1 cup of finely minced vegetables 12 teaspoon ghee

✓   9 pistachios (optional) 4 quarts of water For Seasoning

   Purposes:

✓   1 teaspoon mustard seeds1 curry leaves sprig1

   tablespoon cumin seeds1 gram (1 teaspoon)Bengal 1

   tablespoon black dal

Methodology

1) Heat the oil in a skillet and add the cumin and seeds.

2) Stir in the curry leaves, onion, and green chilies, and observe how the color changes as the leaves cook.

3) Cook until the dal is finely baked in the oil.

4. Pour in some water and bring it to a boil. Season with salt to taste.

5) When cooking, add rice rava on a regular basis.

6) Stir well, cover, and cook over medium-high heat until the humidity is gone.

7) Reduce the heat to low and continue to steam until they are done.

8) Turn off the heat and serve.

Idli Ragi Rava

It helps to protect the bone's integrity and prevents osteoporosis in people with low haemoglobin levels. It contains a good amount of natural fiber and is gluten free. Ragi idli is a very nutritious meal that is great for kids and the elderly. These idlis are soft, spongy, and healthful.

4 individual servings

ingredients

Rice for Idli 2 cups flour 1 cup 1 cup dal 12 teaspoon fenugreek seeds If desired, season with salt.

Following Steps

1) Soak seeds, urad dal, and fenugreek for 4 hours in water. Clean and rinse the rice separately for 5 hours.

2) Grind the dal and seeds till smooth and creamy. Place it in a jar and set it away.

3) Crush the rice to form flour, then mix in the water to make a clearly rough mixture or batter.

4) Stir the rice batter into the dal seed mixture. Mix in the salt and other spices until well blended.

5) The batter's strength should be comparable to that of Idli batter.

6) Using your fingertips, thoroughly blend the wet ingredients.

7) Give it some time to settle. Use a broad vessel to prevent spilling because it can double during fermentation.

8) Our ragi idli batter is complete.

How to Make Ragi Idli

1) Heat the water in a steamer or idle vessel. Mix the soaked ragi idli batter thoroughly, then scoop a dollop of the mixture into the oiled moulds and place them under the broiler.

2) Cook for 20 minutes, or until a toothpick inserted into the idli core comes out clean.

3) After 5 minutes, remove it from the mold with a teaspoon dipped in water.

4) Serve the hot ragi idli with your favorite chutney.

Idli Sabbakki Rava

Time to cook: 12 minutes

15 servings

ingredients

- ✓ 1 cup of Sooji1 teaspoon mustard seeds

- ✓ One teaspoon cumin seeds 1 tbsp Chana dal 1 teaspoon
  black dal (Split) Nuts made from cashews sliced 1/3
  cup 1 sprig curry leaves, shredded Ginger 1 tablespoon
  Asafoetida, if desired 2 chilies, chopped Oil to taste 2
  teaspoons thinly sliced coriander 14 cup Tapioca Perls
  1 cup battered curd lubricating oil

Methodology

1) First, soak the tapioca perls in water for two hours. Filter it and press out the excess water with your fingertips; don't worry if it partially crumbles or loses its shape.

2) Heat the oil in a medium-sized skillet over medium heat. Allow the seeds to vibrate. After a while, add the cumin seeds and dal combination. Mix over a low flame until golden.

3) At this time, add the hinges, curry, ginger, and chilies and simmer for 5 minutes, checking to ensure that the items are thoroughly cooked.

4) This allows the Rava idli mix to be processed and stored in an airtight bag. Add the Rava and roast for 5 minutes before turning off the heat.

5) Heat the water in the idli steamer. Idli moulds should be lubricated.

6) Combine the rava idli mixture, strained tapioca pearls, coriander leaves, salt to taste, and yoghurt in a mixing bowl.

7) Adjust the batter's consistency to a thick one.

8) Fill the idli molds halfway with batter and bake for 15 minutes.

9) Drizzle with olive oil before serving.

Foxtail Millet Rava Idli

Time to cook: 10 minutes

3 servings

3 cups foxtail millet1 cup Fenugreek Seed–14 tablespoons oil, as neededWater as needed. Season with salt to taste.

Methodology

1) Rinse the millet and Urad Dal in separate bowls of water for 6 hours.Fenugreek seeds can be soaked in water alongside the Dal.

2)Separately, crush your millet and daal.

3) In a food processor, grind the soaked dal and fenugreek beans to a fine paste.Place it in a basin. Then, in the same blender, grind the millet that has been submerged. Transfer it, along with the Dal batter, to the basin.

4) Mix the batter together and set it aside to ferment overnight.After fermenting, thoroughly combine all the ingredients.

5) Before cooking, add salt and thoroughly combine. To prepare Idli, add the necessary water to the batter till it reaches the consistency of idli batter. Butter the idli plate and steam for 10 minutes on medium-low heat.

6) Allow it to cool for a few minutes before sprinkling with water and removing the hot idli.

7) To prepare the dosa, add water and adjust the batter to the desired consistency. Heat a dosa tawa and place a dollop of batter onto it, spreading it out evenly. Cook and brush the rim with oil.

8) Before serving, flip and fry the other side.

Dosa with Onion Rava

Time to cook: 15 minutes.

3 individual servings

ingredients

✓ Half a cup of semolina (sooji) 2 tablespoons of
coriander, sliced 1 curry sprig, snipped half a cup rice
flour1 tbsp ginger, finely mincedMaida 14 cup1 chili,
sliced

✓ 1 teaspoon cumin seeds1 thinly sliced onionWherever
possible, use ghee.

Methodology

1) In a cup, combine all of the ingredients, except the
onions, and add water.Use a whisker for quick mixing.

2) Set aside the onions.The batter should be quite thin.

3) If possible, preheat a nonstick dosa plate.It should be warmed up. Drizzle and pour the soupy batter with fat, first forming a bigger ring and then filling the center.

4) Sprinkle the chopped onions on top right away.Mix in a spoonful of oil or ghee. Cook the dosa on a medium flame till it gets golden.

5) Finally, it's time to serve.

Buckwheat Dosa

This healthy and safe dosa is easy to make and is an excellent substitute for bread. Buckwheat has a strong and somewhat nutty flavor that complements a variety of fillings. This recipe calls for the batter to rest for at least overnight so that the flour can be combined with the water. We plan something and make it stand over time so that it can be used the next day.

- ✓ The batter can be refrigerated for up to 2 days.
- ✓ 10 people can be served.
- ✓ Time to cook: 10 minutes.

ingredients

1 cup of buckwheat flour. Oatmeal, 12 cup12 csp almond flour12 teaspoon salt and 12 teaspoon water

Methodology

1) To make a softer batter, combine the buckwheat, oat, and salted almond flour in a mixing bowl. Cover and place the container in the refrigerator at room temperature for at least one night.

2/Pour in the water and thoroughly mix it up.

3) Preheat the Dosa Maker machine to the first setting.

4) Coat the upper and lower frying racks with a thin layer of oil.Pour in a teaspoon of batter.

5) Cook for another 3 minutes.If necessary, open the dosa and cook for 1 minute.

6) Arrange on a plate.

Dhania Palak Dosa

Time to cook: 10 minutes

Individuals: 5

ingredients

2 cups of rice, which must be soaked overnight. 1 cup of dal must be steeped overnight. 1 tsp Fenugreek SeedsSeason with salt to taste. Spinach and coriander leaves, thinly sliced Useful oil

Methodology

1) Wash the rice, spinach, and coriander in water before making the dosa. 2) Allow the rice to be completely immersed in water. Allow it to simmer for six hours.

Soak the dal and fenugreek in water until the dal is completely submerged. Allow them to boil for six hours.

3) After moistening the dal, grind it into a frothy batter.When grinding, only add enough water to make a really soft batter. The batter will appear frothy. Pour the batter into a mixing bowl.

4) Crush the rice into a fairly homogeneous batter, adding just enough water to make it processable.Using a lot of water might make the dosa mixture overly watery. The rice batter can be a little softer, but the dal batter must be exceedingly soft.

5) Combine the dal and rice batter, season with salt to taste, and set aside for at least overnight fermentation.You'll notice that the amount of batter has increased. That is why you can place the batter in a large jar.

6) Make a smooth paste with spinach leaves and coriander in a blender grinder.Set aside.

7). Stir quickly with a spatula until the batter thickens, then season with salt to taste.

8). Stir in the paste and the vegetable mixture until thoroughly combined.

9) Use a few drops of oil to steam a dosa.Lubricate the tawa (pan) with a small amount of oil.

10) Scoop a handful of batter into the center of the tawa.Spread it evenly around the outside in a clockwise motion.

11) Dab a few drops of oil around the edges and in the center of the face.Fry the dosa until the bottom is brown. After that, serve it.

Aval Dosa

Time to cook: 20 minutes.

4 individual servings

three cups rice2 tbsp fenugreek seeds, 1 cup dalSeason with salt and ghee or oil to taste. Water according to specifications

Methodology

1) Separately rinse rice and dal in running water, then cook in containers with just enough salted water.

2) Soak the rice and dal in the bath for at least 6 hours before sleeping.

3) Wash the aval and place it in a clean rice dish filled with water.

(4) In a blender, combine the dal, rice mixture, and fenugreek seeds to make a homogeneous batter.

5) Preheat the oven to 180 degrees Fahrenheit for 15 minutes, then turn it off.

6) Cool the overnight batter in the oven.

7) The next day, season the batter with salt.

8) Heat a dosa tawa and pour a ladle of dosa batter on top.

9) Distribute the range evenly with a slotted spoon.Sprinkle some oil on the sides.

10) Bake until golden brown.

Pohe, Dadpe

3 individual servings

30 minutes of cooking time.

12 cup flattened small rice

1 onion, finely sliced34 cups of grated coconut

two tbsp powdered sugar2-3 tsp lemon zest

Peanuts, raw, three teaspoons

Two tablespoons of coriander leaves

Season with salt to taste.

Three teaspoons of oil

14 tsp. asafetida

Methodology

Combine the finely sliced onions, grated coconut, cinnamon, sugar, and lemon zest.

2) Scatter smooth flattened rice in a bowl and combine at the rim.

3) Heat the cooking oil in a pan over medium heat.Insert the fresh peanuts and fry them before they change color. Remove it and set it aside.

4) To the same hot oil, add the mustard seeds, asafetida, chopped chilies, and curry leaves. 5) Turn off the heat and stir in the turmeric powder. Combine everything thoroughly.

5) Drizzle the finished pohe with this mixture.

6) Perform a quick flip of the entire mixture.

7) Cover and set aside for 10 to 15 minutes to allow the flavors to combine and relax.

8) Serve this delicious Dadpae Pohe for brunch or as a snack any time of day.

Tomato Pohe with Peas

Cooking time: 50 minutes

3 people are served.

ingredients

- ✓ 2 tbsp extra-virgin olive oil
- ✓ 1 large minced onion
- ✓ 1 thinly minced garlic clove
- ✓ 12 cups of sugar, 3 small tomatoes, thinly sliced
- ✓ 1 teaspoon oregano, fresh
- ✓ 1 cup of water, or as needed.
- ✓ 1 tablespoon tomato sauce
- ✓ 1 cup peas, 1 cup zucchini, diced

✓ Salt

Methodology

1) Refresh the poha with just enough water and leave it to soak for 10 minutes.

2/After 10 minutes, completely drain the water, release the poha, and remove any lumps that have formed.

3) Add salt, turmeric powder, lime zest, and red chili powder to taste.

4. Blend thoroughly with a ladle.

5) In a large frying pan or heavy-bottomed saucepan, heat the oil.

6) Add the mustard and cumin seeds and mix well.

7) Let them separate.

8). Stir-fry the onions until they are light brown on medium-low heat. Mix in the vegetables thoroughly.

9)After a few minutes, add the nuts and poha. Cook for 5 minutes, then thoroughly mix.

10) Place in a serving bowl.

11) Serve immediately, garnished with coriander.

Vaghareli of Rotli

Two people can be served.

Time to cook: 30 minutes.

ingredients

- ✓ There are around 4 or 5 chapattis left over.
- ✓ One cup of yoghurt—a great way to use up any extra natural yoghurt in the fridge.
- ✓ 2 teaspoons garlic
- ✓ 1 tablespoon mustard seeds
- ✓ mashed two green chiles
- ✓ a 14th teaspoon turmeric
- ✓ 1 tablespoon of cooking oil.
- ✓ flavorful salt
- ✓ A teeny-tiny bunch of cilantro
- ✓ 1 teaspoon lemon

Methodology

1) Tear the chappatis into bite-sized pieces.

Heat the oil in a saucepan. Turn the heat to medium and add the seeds.

3) Swirl chappati chunks in the oil.

4). Stir in the mustard, turmeric, garlic, and chilies.

5) Stir in a cup and a half of water and the yoghurt until completely combined.

6) Add the chapattis and cook over medium heat.

7) Cook for 5 minutes before adding the sugar and lemon juice.

8) Add the coriander to the mixture and mix well. While the chapattis cook, they will soak up the liquids. If the mixture begins to stick to the bottom of the saucepan, add extra boiling water.

9) The flavor of this dish should be light, with a touch of sweet and sour, so adjust the taste to your liking. Serve it up.

Pohe in Bengali Vegetable Form

Time to cook: 40 minutes.

ingredients

- ✓ You will need the following ingredients to make the batter: maida 12 cups, 12 cups of semolina (sooji)
- ✓ 1 teaspoon of sugar.
- ✓ 1 tablespoon chopped fennel seeds
- ✓ 350ml vacuum-packed milk (as needed for frying)
- ✓ You'll need the following ingredients to make sugar syrup:
- ✓ 1 c. bottled water
- ✓ Four green cardamom pods
- ✓ 1 kilogram of sugar

Methodology

Place all of the batter ingredients in a medium mixing bowl and thoroughly combine them, making sure there are no chunks. If the mixture is too dense, add a little milk. Allow it to rest for a while.

2) In a pot, combine the sugar sauce ingredients and heat until you have one string syrup.

3) In a skillet, heat enough oil to deep fry.

4) Stir a spoon of flour into the liquid to make a little pancake with two diameters.

5) Melt the butter in a skillet over medium heat.Cook and flip one side.

6) If both sides are brown, use a spatula to remove them and immediately immerse them in sugar syrup.Allow 1 minute to fill.

7) Serve immediately after removing from the oven.

Time to cook: 25 minutes.

Two people can be served.

ingredients

- ✓ 14 tbsp. grated beetroot
- ✓ 12 cup whole wheat flour
- ✓ 12 cup gram flour
- ✓ 12 tsp. cumin powder
- ✓ 12 teaspoon amarillo
- ✓ 12 teaspoons of garam masala powder
- ✓ 1 teaspoon Red Chili Oil blend (as needed)
- ✓ Season with salt to taste.

Instructions

Toss the chopped beets with the herbs, salt, and ghee.

2) Gently combine the wheat and besan flours with the water.

3) Form a small portion of the mixture into a thepla.

4) Heat a thepla on a tawa.

5) Heat it for about a minute, then flip it over and heat it for another minute.

6) Serve garnished with curd.

Dhokla Buckwheat Corn

5 individual servings

Time to cook: 35 minutes.

ingredients

- ✓ Two green chiles, minced.

- ✓ 1 piece ginger, chopped

- ✓ 12 teaspoon bicarbonate of soda

- ✓ 1 teaspoon salt (fruit)

- ✓ 12 tsp of turmeric powder

- ✓ 2 tablespoons Sunflower Oil

- ✓ 1/3 cup water

- ✓ 2 cups besan (gram flour)

- ✓ 1 cup of water, or more if available.

- ✓ 2 tablespoons of salt (or to taste)

Method

1: Begin by preparing all of the Dhokla ingredients.

2) Grease a cake tray or dhokla plate and set aside. Prepare a steamer with water and have it ready to go.

3). Next, make a chile and ginger mixture. Combine this mixture and water in a shallow blender mixer container to make a puree. Keep this to yourself.

4) In a large mixing bowl, combine all of the ingredients, including the aforementioned paste, and set aside.

5) Whisk everything together thoroughly, then add the lemon zest and soda to froth up the Dhokla batter.

6) Pour the Dhokla batter into the oiled plate and place it in the steamer.

7) Wrap the steamer, turn on the heat, and steam for 15 minutes.

8) When you stick a knife in the center and down the sides and it comes out dry, you'll know it's done.

9) Remove the Khaman Dhokla from the steamer and place it on a cooling rack to cool completely.

The following step is to prepare the water in the sugar lemon:

10) In a skillet over medium heat, heat the oil.Allow the mustard seeds and cumin seeds to shatter. Mix in the green chilies and curry leaves for about a minute, or until it crackles.

11) When finished, stir in the water, lemon zest, salt, and sugar. Remove it before the sugar dissolves, and then turn off the heat. Allow the tadka to cool somewhat.

12) Spread the tadka over the Khaman Dhokla until evenly coated.

13) Take it out of the pan and serve it.

Crepes with Paneer and green peas

Time to cook: 45 minutes

4 individual servings

ingredients

- ✓ 1 cup fresh green peas
- ✓ 2 cups paneer (cottage cheese made at home)
- ✓ Two tablespoons of ginger, chopped
- ✓ 2 green chilies, chopped
- ✓ 1 tsp turmeric powder
- ✓ 4 tsp. powdered red chili.
- ✓ 2 teaspoons Amchur
- ✓ 2 tablespoons coriander powder

✓ 1 cup whole grain flour

✓ Olive oil is used for kneading.

Methodology

1) Sift the flour into a large mixing bowl. By kneading, add water a few times to make a moist to the puffy dough.

2) Once the dough has formed a circular shape, drizzle with a teaspoon of oil and knead for a few minutes more. We'll wrap the dough, but first we'll make the filling.

3) Heat some oil in a skillet over medium heat. Allow the cumin seeds to sputter for a couple of seconds. Cook it thoroughly after adding all of the seasonings. Put in some peas. Cook until they are halfway done.

4) Stir in the crushed paneer and simmer for a few minutes over medium heat, until the raw flavor of the spice has faded. Allow it to cool.

5) Roll the dough into medium lemon balls.

6) Flour the dough section and pat it down. Roll the dough into a 5-inch-diameter coil. Spoon a large portion of the filling onto the center of the dough.

7. Wrap the ends by drawing them together. Brush the paratha lightly with flour and roll gently to remove any pockets of air.

8) Roll the paratha such that the filling stays inside and does not leak out, resulting in very little strain.

9) The paratha will be cooked next. Preheat the skillet and place the paratha on it.

10) Swap out the surfaces and cook on both before the exterior brown stains appear.Drizzle the paratha with ghee or oil and cook on low to medium heat until the paratha is cooked through and golden brown on both sides.

11) Place the paratha on a plate and repeat with the remaining paneer and green pea packed parathas.

12) Plate it.

Paneer Stuffed Palak with Oats Cheela

Time to cook: 40 minutes.

4 person servings

ingredients

- ✓ 1 kilogram of gram flour
- ✓ 2 to 3 teaspoons oil Ginger-1 teaspoon paste
- ✓ Carom seedlings 14 teaspoon chili powder-14 teaspoon spinach-1 cup (cut thinly)

✓   Add salt to taste.

Methodology

1) First, mix a new batter using the besan chilla and take a spoonful of it.

2) Pour the batter onto a hot griddle.

3) Spread evenly to achieve a somewhat dense chilla.

4) A teaspoon of oil is strewn around the perimeter.

5) Cook for 1 minute on low to medium heat, or until the underside is cooked through.

6) Gently turn the chilla over without splitting it.

7) Make sure to prepare all sides of the chilla.

8). Spread 2 teaspoons of cooked paneer stuffing over a portion of the chilla.

9) Plate it.

CHAPTER 4 : RECIPES FOR INDIAN LUNCH AND DINNER

Lunch and dinner are served with main dish entrees. We may also have a light dinner, but you can still have a good breakfast and a fantastic lunch. This chapter contains a list of such meals that can be served for lunch or dinner. The goal isn't just to share recipes; you may also acquire collection-based ideas and seek out or cook any other dishes that aren't included here.

Madras Chicken Curry

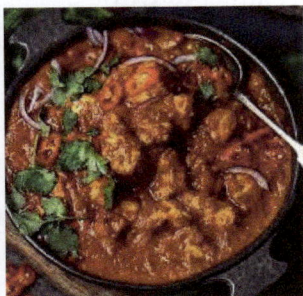

4 people can be served.

Cooking time: 2 hours.

ingredients

- ✓ Ghee-Slathered Onion

- ✓ Coriander Garlic Ginger should be cleaned. Adjust the seasoning to taste.Boneless chicken thighs (no skin) Citrus zest, tomatoes, finely sliced Curry Paste, milk made from coconut

Following Steps

To begin with, heat a large saucepan over medium heat. To the oil, add the sliced onion, chopped garlic, and smashed ginger. Stir for 10 minutes, or until the onions are very soft.

2) Next, add the curry powder, salt, and chili powder. Mix everything together and simmer for a few minutes, or until it gets aromatic.

3) Turn the heat up to medium and add the coconut milk and tomatoes.Cook it for a while.

4) Stir the cut chicken into the gravy, then cover and cook

for 20 minutes.Stir frequently for 25 minutes.

5) Finally, stir in the chopped coriander to finish the

sauce.Sprinkle the lemon zest on top just before serving as

a garnish.

Chicken Tikka Masala Casserole

4 individual servings

Cooking time: 3 hours

ingredients

✓ 8 bone-in chicken thighs

✓ 1 teaspoon lime zest

- ✓ In order to marinate

- ✓ bits of mashed ginger

- ✓ ten mashed garlic cloves

- ✓ Depending on your requirements, yoghurt

- ✓ A pinch of chili powder

- ✓ 1 teaspoon cumin, 1 teaspoon coriander.

- ✓ 1 tbsp garam masala

- ✓ 14 teaspoon turmeric

- ✓ 1 chili, small

Regarding the sauce

- ✓ 1 tbsp. to 12 tbsp. butter

- ✓ 1 finely chopped onion1 teaspoon cumin seeds

- ✓ 1 teaspoon Dijon mustard

- ✓ 12 teaspoons of crushed fenugreek

- ✓ 12 paprika teaspoons

- ✓ 3 cardamoms

- ✓ 1 pound cinnamon slice

- ✓ 1 teaspoon tomato purée

- ✓ 40 g almonds, sliced

- ✓ 1 teaspoon vinegar

- ✓ You can have as much milk as you want.

- ✓ Passata to suit your needs.

Following Steps

1) Remove the skin from the bird and cut each thigh twice or three times.In a plastic jar, combine the chicken pieces, lemon juice, and salt.

Set it aside while you make the seasoning.

In a small spice grinder, crush the ginger and garlic to make a sauce, adding a drop of water if necessary. Set aside a quarter of the paste for the gravy. Add the marinade ingredients to the spice grinder and grind to a fine paste.

3) Pour the mixture over the chicken in a jar and set aside for at least 4 hours to marinate.

(4) In a deep skillet, heat 2 tablespoons of ghee over medium heat to render the sauce. Cook the onions for 20 minutes over medium heat before they begin to brown.

5) Cook for 5 minutes after adding the spices and the leftover garlic and ginger paste. Make a sauce with tomatoes, almonds, and vinegar. Warm it up for a few minutes.

6) Pour in the passata, then halfway fill the container with water.Set it to a low heat and cook it for 2-3 hours, or until a thick sauce forms. It can be frozen in the refrigerator for up to 24 hours while the chicken marinates.

7) Preheat the grill to the highest possible setting.

8) Arrange a chicken on a large baking sheet, cut-side up.Set aside 10-15 minutes under the grill before charring and blackening. Remove the baking sheet from the oven.

9) Reheat the sauce and brush the remaining marinade and curry sauce over the chicken.Cook until the chicken is completely cooked through. Allow the curry to rest for a few minutes.

10) Before serving, garnish with cilantro and almonds.

Saag Aloo with Beef Kofta

4 people can be served.

1 hour of cooking time.

ingredients

- ✓ A single onion
- ✓ 1 clove garlic
- ✓ Two medium-sized potatoes
- ✓ 12 bunch coriander
- ✓ one-quarter teaspoon cumin
- ✓ 12 teaspoons of turmeric
- ✓ 12 tsp. of mustard
- ✓ 1 pot for reserving chicken
- ✓ 300 g beef, ground
- ✓ Depending on your requirements, you can use coconut milk.
- ✓ 12 teaspoons of lemon zest (optional)

Following Steps

1) To begin, cut and slice the onion into small pieces.Grind the garlic once it has been sliced.

Make cubes out of the potatoes. Cut the coriander into small pieces.

Heat the oil in a large frying pan over medium heat. Cook for 5 minutes, or until the garlic and onion become soft. Half of this stuff should be kept aside in a tray.

3) In a frying pan, combine the remaining onion, cumin, turmeric, and mustard and cook for 3 minutes.

4). Add the potato cubes and water to taste, as well as half a pot of chicken stock. Mix it thoroughly so that it dissolves. Cook for about 15-20 minutes, covered with a lid on a low heat.

5) In the meantime, season the meat in a bowl with salt, black pepper, and crushed garlic.

6) For each person, divide the meat mixture into four small balls.Heat oil in a frying pan over medium heat until golden brown all over.

7) Remove the koftas from the pan.

8) Carefully drop the koftas into the boiling liquid.

9) Remove the spinach from the heat, cover with a lid, and set aside for 10 minutes.Combine it with the spinach. Pour in a little lemon zest and mix it in well. Serve it up.

Curry with Mangoes and Chicken

4 people can be served.

Time to cook: 2 hours.

ingredients

✓   2 teaspoons coconut oil

- ✓ 1 large onion, chopped4 garlic cloves.

- ✓ 8 teaspoons ginger, minced

- ✓ 4 teaspoons curry powder

- ✓ Season with salt and pepper to taste.

- ✓ 3 mangos, sliced, diced, and split

- ✓ Depending on your needs, you can use coconut milk.

- ✓ 2-4 chicken thighs, sliced

Following Steps

1) Melt the coconut oil in a large, deep fryer over medium heat.

Cook the onion, garlic, and ginger until they are brown.

2) Combine the curry powder, salt, pepper, 1 cup of the fresh mangoes, and coconut milk in a large mixing bowl.

3) Next, add the above-mentioned sauce to the frying pan along with the chicken and 12 cups of water. Cook for 20 minutes, covered with a lid.

Reduce the heat if the frying pan's edge begins to cling to the sauce.

4) When all of the chicken parts are cooked, add the remaining mango to the plate and serve.

Sandwich with Tandoori Curry

4 people can be served.

1 hour of cooking time.

ingredients

✓ 1 whole chicken, chopped into bite-sized portions

✓ 1 cup plain Greek yogurt

✓ 12 yellow onions, chopped

- ✓ 1 ginger, peeled and grated

- ✓ 2 garlic cloves

- ✓ 2 tbsp. healthy citrus juice

- ✓ 12 tablespoon cumin

- ✓ 12 teaspoons of cilantro powder

- ✓ 1 tablespoon of olive oil

- ✓ potatoes and salt.

To make large sandwiches, use half-warm whole wheat bread.

- ✓ Greek yoghurt (regular)

- ✓ 1 tablespoon cumin seed

- ✓ 12 teaspoons of cilantro powder

- ✓ 14 tsp. garlic powder

- ✓ Tomatoes and salt

- ✓ Lettuce

Following Steps

1)Place the chicken pieces in a large zip-lock bag.

2) Blend the milk, onion, ginger, garlic, lemon juice, cumin, coriander, and oil in a food processor until smooth.Season with salt and pepper to taste.

3)Place the chicken and sauce in a zip-lock bag and shake to coat. Simply marinate the chicken in the fridge for at least 4 hours.

4) Preheat the oven to 500 degrees F.Place the bird on the rack, skin side down. Roast for 35 minutes, or until burnt areas appear on the chicken, tossing once. Reduce the heat to 450°F and continue to cook for another 10 minutes, or until the chicken is totally done.

5). If desired, dice the remaining chicken into bite-size pieces.

6) In a shallow bowl, combine the yoghurt and spices. each pita half to form a pocket and filling it with meat, lettuce, tomato sauce, and yoghurt,

Butter Curry Chicken with Veggie Filling

Serves three people

2 hours of cooking time.

ingredients

- ✓ 2 tbsp. melted butter
- ✓ 1 large diced white onion
- ✓ Two large garlic cloves
- ✓ 1 teaspoon freshly grated ginger

- ✓ 1 tsp. Garam Masala

- ✓ 1 tablespoon curry powder

- ✓ 1 teaspoon powdered cilantro

- ✓ 12 teaspoon paprika

- ✓ 14 teaspoon ground cinnamon

- ✓ Flakes of chili, around 14 tablespoons

- ✓ A pair of tomatoes

- ✓ 1 bottle (400 mL) coconut milk

Following Steps

1. Melt the coconut oil or butter in a large skillet or pot over medium-low heat. Cook for about 6 minutes, or until the onion is transparent.

2) Sauté garlic and ginger for 5 minutes, or until aromatic, before adding garam masala, curry powder, cilantro, paprika, and cinnamon.Allow it to simmer for about 1 minute, swirling occasionally.

3) Half-fill the container with chili flakes and tomatoes.Allow the sauce to simmer for about 15 minutes, or until the sauce thickens and turns a strong and rich red-brown color.

4) Remove from the heat and place in a blender.Season with salt to taste. If the mixture is too heavy to include, add up to a quarter cup of water. If you have a small blender, blend in batches.

5) Put the sauce back in the tub.Pour in the coconut milk and sugar.

At this point, add your prepared lentils, tomatoes, chickpeas, and vegan chicken and simmer for 10-15 minutes.

6) Use corn and coriander to represent it.

Pulao with paneer

4 people can be served.

Time to cook: 2 hours.

ingredients

- ✓ 1 cup of basmati rice

- ✓ 1 and a half Paneer cubes

- ✓ a half-cup of carrots and peas

- ✓ A single big onion

- ✓ 2 green peppers

- ✓ a teaspoon of garlic and gingerPaste coriander leaves, diced as desired.

- ✓ As needed, salt

✓   Ghee or oil

Following Steps

Rinse and soak the rice for around 30 minutes. Heat the ghee in a saucepan over medium heat for 3 minutes. Add the well-drained soaked rice and cook for a few minutes, or until it is dry.

2) In a skillet over medium heat, heat the oil.Fry the onion and green chile until the onion is barely transparent and the color has not changed.

3) Add the ginger and garlic paste, fry it, and then add the vegetables. Fry them until they are half-finished.

4) Add 1 cup of water and salt and set aside to cook.Cooked rice should be added now. Cook over a low flame, covered with a lid.

5) Cut the paneer into cubes. For a richer flavor, leave it overnight.the paneer cubes to be tiny. Paneer cubes (thawed or submerged in hot water) are commonly roasted in a nonstick skillet till golden brown.

6) When the pulao is done, drain the paneer and mix it in with the pulao.Before adding, make sure the pavé is completely dry.

Dal Makhni

4 people can be served.

Time to cook: 2 hours.

ingredients

- ✓ 2 tbsp red beans, soaked overnight
- ✓ 1 teaspoon red chili powder
- ✓ 8 tablespoons of melted butter
- ✓ 1 large diced onion
- ✓ Half a cup of tomato puree.
- ✓ 12 quarts fresh milk
- ✓ half a teaspoon ginger paste
- ✓ Add salt as needed.
- ✓ two slices of ginger
- ✓ Two huge chopped chilies 12 cups of dal, soaked in water overnight.
- ✓ a half teaspoon garlic paste

Following Steps

Soak the dal in two cups of water overnight. Cook it in a pressure cooker with salt and 3 cups of water. This causes the dal and rajma to soften.

2) Heat the cumin seeds in a pan over medium heat.After some cooking, add the ginger and garlic paste slowly until the cumin seeds rasp and swirl. Then, add some carrots, chopped green chilies, and tomato puree.

3). Fry the mixture before it turns golden. If you prefer the true appearance of Dal Makhani, we recommend using ghee instead of oil.

4) Once the masala is to your liking, add the Rajma and dal and let it to steam.

5) Season to taste with garam masala and salt.Transfer it to a pot and stir well; if the dal seems too dense, add more water.

6) Stir in some fresh cream until fully combined. This will result in a creamy and flavorful Dal Makhani.

Lemon Chicken

4 people can be served.

Time to cook: 2 hours.

ingredients

- ✓ 1 teaspoon lemon zest, 1 teaspoon honey

- ✓ 1 cup olive oil

- ✓ 2 minced garlic cloves.

- ✓ 1 teaspoon oregano, crushed

- ✓ To eat, a fresh green salad with potatoes

Following Steps

1) Preheat the gas furnace to 170°C. Arrange the chicken in a single layer on a large baking sheet.

2) In a small skillet or oven, combine all of the ingredients and cook for 1 minute.Remove everything at once, then pour over the chicken.

3) Grill the chicken for 45 minutes, turning every 10 minutes.

The fluid thickens gradually, providing a glossy coating to the chicken.

4) Remove the chicken from the oven and set aside for 5 minutes before serving with a green salad and fresh potatoes.

Chettinad Trout Fry

Two people serving

Time to cook: 2 hours.

ingredients

- ✓ 400g of fish.

- ✓ 1 tbsp turmeric powder

- ✓ season with salt to taste

- ✓ 1 tablespoon lemon juice

- ✓ three onions

- ✓ 2 cloves garlic

- ✓ 2 teaspoons of fresh ginger.

- ✓ Cumin seeds, 2 tablespoons

- ✓ 2 tablespoons rice flour
- ✓ According to your requirements,
- ✓ 1 teaspoon red chili powder
- ✓ 1 tbsp. coriander powder

Following Steps

1) Wash the fish in water after cutting it into bite-sized pieces.

2) Sprinkle with turmeric powder, salt, and lemon juice before covering and storing.

3) Fill the blender jar halfway with cumin seeds, garlic, ginger, and onion, and blend until smooth. combine to produce a paste.

4) Transfer the masala mixture to a skillet and add the red chili powder, coriander powder, rice flour, salt, and two tablespoons of oil to make a dense paste.

5) Remove the fish portions and apply an even layer of masala paste to the fish.

6) Marinate the fish in the marinade for 2 hours.

7) Then, in a grill pan or skillet, heat the oil.

8) When the oil is heated enough, add the fish pieces one at a time and fry until they are done on one side before turning to the next.

9) Pat the fish dry with a clean cloth to remove excess fat.

10) Serve with a cup of hot, freshly cooked rice on the side.

Mutton Pyaaza (Mutton Do Pyaaza)

Two people serving

1 hour of cooking time.

ingredients

- ✓ Mutton (half a kilogram)

- ✓ 12 cups of yogurt

- ✓ Cardamom seeds

- ✓ 5 chili peppers, or to taste.

- ✓ 1/2 tsp cinnamon powder

- ✓ half a teaspoon cumin

- ✓ 1 teaspoon garlic pulp

- ✓ Season with salt to taste.

- ✓ 1 teaspoon cayenne pepper

- ✓ 12 teaspoon turmeric

- ✓ 12 cup olive oil

- ✓ 3 onions, diced.

- ✓ A teaspoon of poppy seeds

- ✓ A teaspoon of coconut sand

Following Steps

1) Clean the meat while keeping the strainer in place.

2) Combine yoghurt, cardamom, cinnamon powder, chiles, cumin, garlic paste, salt, red chili powder, and turmeric.

3) Pour the mixture over the meat and set aside for an hour.

4) Heat the oil in a skillet and sauté the onion until it is lightly golden in color. Remove the onion from the pan and continue to cook the meat in the same pan.

5) When the water in the yoghurt runs out, substitute enough liquid to cook the meat. Cook, covered, until the vegetables are soft.

6) Combine the coconut and poppy seeds in a mixing bowl.

7). Cook for 2 minutes after adding the fried onion. and then serve it.

Makhmali Kofte (Makhmali Kofte)

serves three people.

Time to cook: 2 hours.

ingredients

- ✓ To make the Koftas, combine the following ingredients:
- ✓ 400g of sliced Indian cottage cheese (Paneer)
- ✓ Two large potatoes, cooked and mashed
- ✓ 2 green chilies, chopped
- ✓ 14 teaspoon ground white pepper
- ✓ 2 heaping tablespoons corn flour
- ✓ 4 tbsp oil for preparation
- ✓ To taste, add salt.

- ✓ To make the gravy, follow these steps:
- ✓ a fourth cup of oil
- ✓ 2 medium sliced onions
- ✓ 1 tablespoon grated ginger
- ✓ Cut half a garlic plant.
- ✓ 20 cashews, soaked in water for 10 minutes
- ✓ 1 cup tomato puree
- ✓ 1 dark cardamom
- ✓ Gray 3 cardamom
- ✓ ONE BAY LEAF
- ✓ 1 teaspoon ground cinnamon
- ✓ half a teaspoon chili powder
- ✓ 2 teaspoons milk
- ✓ 1 teaspoon Kasuri methi is also known as fenugreek.
- ✓ To taste, add salt.

Following Steps

1) Combine all of the ingredients (except the oil) and roll them into balls.

2) In a large skillet, heat the oil and fry the koftas until golden brown on both sides.

3) Set aside half of the chopped onion

4) Fry them in heated oil until they are beautifully browned.

5) In a food processor, make a fine paste with the leftover onions, ginger, garlic, and cashews.

6) Heat the oil in a shallow pan and add the garam masala, black and green cardamom, garlic, bay leaf, and cinnamon.

7) As the spices change color, add the paste. Cook for 3 minutes on high heat.

8) Stir in the fried onion for 5 minutes.

9) Stir in a tomato puree, red Kashmiri chili, and salt. Cook for 20 minutes on a low heat with a glass of water.

10) When the mixture has cooled slightly, gently fold in the cream and methi.

11) Pour the sauce into a large, deep basin. Lower the koftas into the sauce one at a time, being careful not to stack them on top of one another.

12) Finish with a light sprinkle of cream. Serve with caution.

Masala Pasta

serves three people.

1 hour of cooking time

ingredients

- ✓ 1 cup pasta (choose your favorite)
- ✓ 1 teaspoon olive oil
- ✓ 1 tablespoon cumin seeds
- ✓ 3 sliced garlic cloves
- ✓ 1 onion, thinly sliced
- ✓ 3 thinly sliced, chopped tomatoes
- ✓ 1 tablespoon turmeric powder
- ✓ 1 teaspoon curry powder of choice
- ✓ 1 tbsp. coriander powder
- ✓ Depending on your preference, grind red chili.
- ✓ season with salt to taste
- ✓ 1 cup of water (or as needed).

Steps to Take

1) Preheat an electric skillet to high heat for stir-frying.Allow the oil to warm up before adding it to the pan.

2) Cook for a few minutes after adding the garlic, onions, and cumin seed.

3). Stir in the tomatoes and simmer until they are soft. Mix in all of the dried spices and salt.

4) Fry for a minute or two.

5) Add the pasta and water.After thoroughly mixing, turn off the stir fry mode.

6) Hold the ventilation to the sealing point for 7 minutes on high mode. Unlock it after 10 minutes.

7) Plate it to your liking.

Mushrooms with Garlic

Serves three people

1 hour of cooking time.

ingredients

- ✓ 2 teaspoons melted butter

- ✓ 2 tablespoons of olive oil

- ✓ 1/4 cup thinly chopped onion

- ✓ 1 cup shiitake mushrooms, button mushrooms

- ✓ 2 tablespoons finely ground garlic

✓ fresh, split, and thinly sliced peaches, a couple of tablespoons parsley

✓ 12 teaspoons each of thyme and oregano, finely minced. 12 tablespoons of new red chili flakes, finely chopped to taste.

Following Steps

1) Heat oil and butter in a nonstick skillet over low to moderate heat.

2) Stir in the onions and cook for 3 minutes.

3) Add the mushrooms and cook until they are light brown.

4) Stir in all of the spices and simmer well.

5) Cook till it has a garlic flavor. Take care not to burn the garlic.

6) Stir in the remaining parsley, then remove from the heat and serve

CHAPTER 5:RECIPES FOR INDIAN DESSERTS

Dessert is the finishing touch on a platter. Desserts, without a doubt, provide a satisfying finale to any dinner. It's no surprise that individuals have a fondness for sweets and desserts. Deserts are not only a mainstay of our diet, but they are also provided in many places of worship. Sugar, milk, and khoya are widely used as essential ingredients in all Indian desserts.

Falooda Shahi

ingredients

- ✓ two milk bottles

- ✓ two tablespoons rice

- ✓ Honey, 2 tbsp

- ✓ 2 teaspoons flavoring syrup

- ✓ two tablespoons finely minced dry fruits of your choice

  and preference

Following Steps

1) Cook the rice in water for about 15 minutes, then strain and leave aside to cool.

In a mixer, combine the milk, sugar, and dry fruit and blend until smooth.

3) Pile rice into two glasses, one on top of the other.

4) Pour in half of the milk now. After adding the syrup, each of them should be blended thoroughly and chilled in the refrigerator.

5) If you want to use ice cream, mix in an ice cream scoop and season with dried berries. Connect a long-handled serve.

Jamun Gulab Jamun

For the dough balls:

- ✓ 1 cup sweetened condensed milk

- ✓ 110 g plain flour

- ✓ 1 and 1/2 teaspoons baking powder

- ✓ half a teaspoon baking soda

- ✓ 1 and a half cup milk

- ✓ 25g of hot sugar

- ✓ frying oil

To make a syrup, combine the following ingredients:

- ✓ 1 cup of caster sugar

- ✓ Saffron, to taste, 100ml water

- ✓ As a garnish:

- ✓ 1 tbsp. chopped pistachio nut.

In a skillet, heat 1 tablespoon roasted almonds.

Steps to take

1) In any bowl for the dough balls, combine all of the ingredients, adding enough extra water to form a smooth, sticky dough.

Set aside for 20 minutes, covered. Cut the dough into small, spherical pieces.

2) In a deep fryer with thick sides, heat the oil. Fry the balls in it until they are light brown, then scrape the oil out with a serving dish and set aside to drain.

3) Make a sugar syrup by boiling the sugar, water, and saffron together.

4) Once the dough balls are cooked, place them in the sugar fluid and soak for about an hour.

5) Garnish with nuts and almonds before serving.

Kulfi

✓ *ingredients*

- ✓ 1 liter full-fat milk
- ✓ half a cup thick cream
- ✓ 1/3 cup khoya crushed
- ✓ 1 tablespoon dry milk powder (for flavor)

- ✓ 3 tbsp cashew/pistachio mixture

- ✓ 10 teaspoons sugar

- ✓ Five green cardamoms separated and smashed the skin.

Following Steps

1) Heat the entire milk in a heavy center pan over a low or medium temperature.

2) Stir in the cream after about 10 minutes, as it begins to heat up.

3) Allow the solution to simmer for a few minutes before reducing the heat to low.

4) Boil the milk for about 25 minutes on low heat, stirring regularly.

5) After about 25-30 minutes, the milk will be quite thick; at this time, add the crushed khoya and combine. Continue to whisk for 10 minutes, or until the khoya has melted.

6) When the khoya has melted, add the sugar and continue to cook until it dissolves.

7) Finally, add the previously cut nuts. The finely chopped nuts give the kulfi extra texture.

8) Stir in the condensed milk. Cook for an additional 5 minutes. It should be very thick at the end, and it will continue to thicken as it cools.

9) Remove the pan from the heat and stir in the cardamom powder. Allow it to cool.

10) Once the milk has completely chilled, pour it into kulfi molds or any suitable jar. Cover and place in the freezer until fully grown.

11) After the kulfi mould has frozen, rinse it with warm, clean water and tap it on the counter. The kulfi will soon fall out. Enjoy the delectable Kulfi malai.

Doi Mishti

ingredients

- ✓ 1 liter creamed milk

- ✓ 8 Cardamom Curd according to taste

- ✓ 1 cup of sugar, or as desired

Following Steps

1) In a large nonstick saucepan, heat one liter of cream milk.

2) Continuously stir it while boiling the milk.

3) Stir in a cup of sugar until fully combined.

4) Heat the milk over a low flame until it thickens. Stir on a regular basis until the milk has reduced to half of its original volume. In the meantime, heat two tablespoons brown sugar in a saucepan. Blend it properly after adding the water. Stir until the sugar dissolves, keeping the heat on low.

5) Adding the caramel sugar to the heating milk.

6) Stir thoroughly and transfer the milk to the next boil. Allow it to cool completely. After the milk has chilled but is still little moist, transfer it to a clay pot or another jar.

7) Add a teaspoon of curd and mix thoroughly.

8) Cover and leave aside for 8 hours in a warm place, or until completely set.

9) Refrigerate for 2 hours to achieve a creamy texture. It can also be sweetened with sliced nuts.

10) Finally, serve the mishti doi cooled.

Desert of Indian Cham Cham

ingredients

- ✓ 4 cups of cream milk
- ✓ Paneer, did you prepare this before or did you take it?
- ✓ readymade
- ✓ 2 cups sugar
- ✓ 5 quarts of water
- ✓ 1/8 teaspoon cardamom powder

Following Steps

1) First, prepare the paneer. Take a little piece of paneer in your hand and rub it with your fingertips to see if enough water has been drained from it. After 30 seconds of pressing, a firm yet smooth surface is created.

2) Place the soaked paneer on a flat, level surface and knead for 3 to 4 minutes, or until it forms a smooth, soft dough. If the paneer is too mushy, add a teaspoon of water.

3) Divide the paneer dough into eight equal sections and shape each into a flat oval face disc.

4) To make the syrup, bring 5 cups of water to a boil in a big pot. Whisk in the sugar until it is completely dissolved. As the Chum Chum doubles in volume when cooking in the syrup, use a large pan.

5) Return the paneer balls to the syrup and swirl to incorporate.

Then reduce the flame to medium and cover with foil. 15 minutes in the oven

6) Remove the pan's lid, turn the chum chums over, and cook for another 15 minutes. Examine how the chum chums appear solid yet sponge-like. Turn off the flame and leave it alone for 10 minutes.

7) Keep chum chums out of the water. After chilling, represent it.

Sitaphal

✓ *ingrediants*

✓ 1 cup freshly peeled custard apple pulp (eliminated seeds)

- ✓ 2 large white eggs

- ✓ chilled cream milk (400 mL)

- ✓ a third cup powdered sugar

- ✓ a third teaspoon vanilla extract

Following Steps

1) In a large bowl, crush the custard apple to a gritty pulp using a blade.

2) While the Sitaphal is freezing, in a dry container, beat the two egg whites with a hand beater until they become fuzzy and have soft tips. The key is to gently separate the egg white.

And even a trace of yolk prevents the whites from becoming soft.

3) In a small bowl, combine the water, butter, and essence. If you whisk too forcefully, the cream will turn to butter.

4) Add the custard apple pulp to the milk mixture and combine with a spoon.

5) Gently fold this mixture into the egg whites. The goal is to keep as much air as possible in the egg whites in order to make silky, creamy, and tasty ice cream. Place in a frozen basin after all prepared.

6) Allow it stand for 3 hours in the freezer. Remove from the refrigerator and stir again until smooth.

7) Place it back in the fridge and refrigerate it again. Scroll out into and feed individual pots.

Til Ladu

ingredients

- ✓ 500 grams of flour
- ✓ 1 liter of milk or other beverage
- ✓ Ghee (750 g)
- ✓ Sugar (750 g)
- ✓ 3 quarts of water
- ✓ 5–10 drops orange coloring
- ✓ 10 to 12 saturated saffron flakes
- ✓ 50 sliced cashews
- ✓ You can use as many raisins as you want.
- ✓ 12 cardamom pods

Following Steps

1) Make a thin combination of water and gram flour/milk.

In a saucepan, melt the ghee.

2) Pour up to half of the batter into the frying pan or sieve.

3) Place it over a pan of hot ghee and drain the boondis by striking the strainer against the side of the tub, picking it up, and hitting it again. The next phase should be rather simple.

4) Fry them till they are the color of gold. Using the batter all over the place.

5) Prepare sugar syrup with a threaded thickness of one and a half threads by heating sugar and water.

6) Color the syrup with saffron water. Combine the boondis, cardamom, dried fruits, and honey in a mixing bowl. And thoroughly combine it.

7) After 10 minutes, sprinkle with hot water, cover, and leave for 12 hours.

8) Form it into circular spheres with wet hands.

Brittle with Peanuts from India

- ✓ 1 cup roasted peanuts (skin free).
- ✓ 1 cup of sugar Following Steps
- ✓ In a blender, puree the peanuts until they form a homogeneous paste.

Following Steps

Place a pan with the sugar and 2 spoons of water on a medium heat. Continue to stir. The sugar gradually turns into caramel.

2) Once all of the lumps have melted, remove them from the pan and thoroughly blend in the peanut

powder.Transfer the paste to a grating dish and distribute evenly.

3) While the paste is still hot, make lines with a knife and set aside to cool.

4) Once cold, cut into squares along with the guidelines.

Barfi in India

ingredients

✓ 2 cups granules creamy milk

- ✓ Approximately 300ml of hard cream
- ✓ 400 g of sweetened condensed milk, 400 g
- ✓ 1/2 cup finely sliced pistachios

Following Steps

1) Begin by gathering all of the ingredients.

2/Whisk together all of the milk and cream until smooth.

3) Cover the pan and place it in the microwave for about 8 minutes.

4) Keep an eye on the dish and, if the solution appears to be on the verge of boiling over, stop the microwave for 8 to 10 seconds.

Begin again and work until the time limit of 8 minutes has been met. Take it out and thoroughly combine it.

5) Return the pan to the microwave for another 8 minutes on high.

Allow the cooking to commence after carefully monitoring the first minute.

6) When the timer goes off, scatter the sliced pistachios over the surface of the barfi and set aside for 10 minutes.

7) After 10 minutes, remove the barfi from the microwave and cut it into 2-inch squares. Allow it to cool before serving.

Rice Pudding from India

ingredients

✓ half a cup rice

- ✓ 3 quarts full-fat milk

- ✓ 1 quart coconut milk

- ✓ half a cup sugar

- ✓ 1 teaspoon cardamom (green)

- ✓ 1 tablespoon of oil

- ✓ A heaping tablespoon of cashews

- ✓ 1 tbsp chopped pistachios

- ✓ 1 tbsp almonds (all nuts should be blanched)

- ✓ chopped

- ✓ Saffron, 1 teaspoon

Following Steps

1) Begin by gathering all of your ingredients.

2) If you wish to shorten the cooking time, soak the rice for 30 minutes before using it. Not only does this shorten the boiling time, but it also uses up to half as much milk.

3) If using whole cardamom pods, coarsely grind them with a pestle and mortar. Add the nuts and crush them to a fine pulp.

4) Bring the milk, coconut milk, and rice to a boil in a large pot. Reduce the heat to low and add the sugar and cardamom to steam. To warm the butter. Continuously stir it.

5) Cook, stirring frequently, until the rice is smooth and not rubbery. The cooking time will vary approximately 1 hour depending on the rice you've been using. Keep an eye on the mixture while it warms, and add additional sugar if it becomes too hot.

6) Assemble your desired toppings and toast the nuts in rice.

7) Allow it to cool. After that, serve it.

Jalebi

- ✓ 1 cup all-purpose flour

- ✓ 1 tbsp. chickpea starch

- ✓ 14 teaspoon cardamom powder

- ✓ a tsp of baking powder

- ✓ 14 tsp of baking soda

- ✓ yoghurt (five teaspoons)

- ✓ If you like, you can use orange food coloring.

- ✓ Water as needed.

- ✓ Fry the jalebi in oil or ghee.

- ✓ **Jalebi syrup for dipping**

✓ 1 kilogram of sugar

✓ 12 cups of water, 1/4 teaspoon of cardamom powder, and 12 teaspoons of lemon extract.

Following Steps

1) Mix together all of the ingredients.

2) Focus on making a long-lasting batter, then add food coloring and water to it.

3) The batter should be light and fluffy.Depending on the consistency of the maida and besan, up to 3/4 of the water may be required.

4) Wrap the batter in foil and leave it to ferment for 10 hours.

5) After that, whisk in a little extra batter.If the batter is too thick at this point, add a bit more water.

In the meantime, add water to the mixture, followed by sugar, and allow it to simmer.

7) Allow the syrup to steam until it thickens and becomes sticky.Simply place a drop of syrup between your thumb and forefinger, and as you move your fingers away from one another, it should form a uniform thread.

8) Pour the batter into a container.

9) Melt the butter or ghee in a pan.Reduce the heat to medium-low.

10) Squeeze the batter into the hot oil, allowing the spiral to go through.It's important to keep the shape at a low temperature, or you won't be able to create it. If the batter disperses in the oil, it is probably too thin and needs extra flour. After you've formed the spiral form with the batter, increase the heat to moderate to high.

11) Fry until it's crispy. Remove from the oil and dip into the warm sugar syrup for a couple of seconds on each side.

Remove the jalebis from the sugar syrup and place them on the serving tray. Serve the homemade jalebi with rabri or milk. Any almonds on top should be garnished.

Shakkarpara

✓ *ingredients*

- ✓ 2 processed flour tassels

- ✓ 14 cup of ghee

- ✓ 1 cup of sugar

- ✓ Ghee

Following Steps

1) To make the shakarparas dough, begin by grinding the processed flour.

2) Combine processed flour and a quarter cup melted ghee in a mixing bowl.Mix everything up thoroughly. Fill it with water. During the winter, you can knead the flour with warm water. To knead the same amount of dough, we used half a cup of water. Cover the dough and set it aside for a half-hour to rest.

3) Re-knead the dough after 20 minutes to make it smoother and fluffier.Separate the dough into two pieces.

To prevent it from drying out, take one half and cover it with the other. Form it into a flat dough disc first.

4. Remove the sheet that is now being stored. Second, from the corners, smooth out the stretched sheet. Then cut it into wide pieces. Cut the stripes into long strips. You can keep the size as large or as small as you need.Separate the shakarparas and lay them on a tray.

Re-enact the procedure.

5) In a skillet, heat enough oil to fry those.Drop one piece of shakarpara into the ghee to test it. To cook the shakarparas, we don't need very hot ghee; it should be moderately heated. Maintain a medium-low flame. When the ghee is completely hot, add the rest of the shakarparas.

6) When the shakarparas rise to the surface, flip them over and fry until golden on all sides.Strain the cooked

shakarparas in a pan. Maintain the skillet on the wok's edge so that any extra ghee drains back into the wok.

7) Collect a container for making sugar syrup.Pour in the sugar and water.

Cook until the sugar dissolves. To taste, place a few drops in a bowl and place your thumb and index finger in between them. When the fingers are extended apart, see if a lengthy string forms. The syrup has hardened. Turning off the flame

8) Place this jar over a net stand so that the syrup condenses a little. Drop the shakarparas into the sugar syrup and cover them nicely when the syrup becomes small and dense in consistency—after combining the shakarparas in the syrup, remove the shakarparas immediately from the syrup and place them in a large basin. Empty the excess syrup into the same container. If the syrup becomes too thick when coating the shakarparas, reheat it slightly.

9) Stir a spoon of sugar-coated shakarparas to separate

it.They'd cling to each other.

CHAPTER 6: VEGETARIAN INDIAN RECIPES

Nowadays, more people prefer to consume exclusively vegetarian food rather than nonvegetarian food because most nonvegetarian dishes increase the amount of fat in our bodies and take a long time to digest due to specific health issues such as obesity, thyroid, and weight gain. In this chapter, you will learn about various vegetarian foods that are both nutritious and delicious.

Biryani with vegetables.

serves three people.

Time to cook: 2 hours.

ingredients

- ✓ 2 tbsp extra-virgin olive oil

- ✓ One small cauliflower, divided into little pieces.

- ✓ 2 large sweet potatoes, peeled and cut into cubes.

- ✓ 1 large onion, sliced

- ✓ One supply of spicy vegetables.

- ✓ A spoonful of curry paste

- ✓ 1 chili, finely sliced

- ✓ A generous pinch of saffron threads

- ✓ 1 teaspoon mustard seeds

- ✓ 500 g rice

- ✓ Beans, 140 g

- ✓ 2 tablespoons lemon juice

- ✓ A couple of coriander leaves

Following Steps

1) In a large deep pan over medium heat, melt the

ghee.Add the onion and cook for about 5 minutes, or until

soft. Mix in the cumin seeds and simmer for about 5 minutes, or until the cumin seeds begin to explode.

2) Combine the ginger-garlic-onion paste and 12 cups of sugar in a mixing bowl.Bring it to a boil and cook for 5 minutes, or until the water is absorbed.

Mix in the peas, onions, and carrots. Also, mix in all of the spices. Stir it carefully, then cover it with a lid and leave it to simmer for three minutes.

3) Bring 4 cups of water to a boil over medium heat.

After the rice has boiled, decrease the heat to low, re-heat, and simmer for 10 minutes. Reduce the heat to low and continue to cook for another 20 minutes, or until the rice has softened.

Indian Sparkling Wine with Dhal

4 people can be served.

1 hour of cooking time.

ingredients

- ✓ 1 teaspoon olive oil

- ✓ 1 cup sliced onion

- ✓ 2 garlic cloves, finely chopped

- ✓ 1 tbsp ginger (roughly chopped)

- ✓ 4 quarts of water.

- ✓ 1 cup washed dried red lentils

- ✓ 1 tablespoon cumin

- ✓ 1 tablespoon of coriander (cilantro)

- ✓ a 14th teaspoon turmeric

- ✓ A quarter teaspoon of cardamom

- ✓ 14 teaspoon ground cinnamon

- ✓ 14 teaspoon ground black pepper

- ✓ Season with salt to taste.

- ✓ two tbsp tomato paste

Following Steps

1) Begin by gathering all of the ingredients.

2) In a medium-sized soup pan, heat the oil over medium heat.

Mix in the onion, garlic, and ginger. Cook, stirring frequently, for about 6 minutes.

3) Combine the water, lentils, vegetables, and salt in a mixing bowl.Continue to stir constantly.

Bring the soup to a low boil, then reduce to a low heat, cover, and cook for 20 minutes, or until the lentils are very soft.

(4) When everything is completely combined, add the tomato paste. Cook for a few minutes longer.

5) Serve and enjoy yourself.

Cabbage Koora

4 people can be served.

Time to cook: 2 hours.

ingredients

- ✓ 3 tablespoons cooking oil
- ✓ 2 dried hot chili peppers, sliced into pieces.
- ✓ 1 tablespoon split black-skinned lentils
- ✓ 1 tablespoon Bengal gram
- ✓ 1 teaspoon mustard seeds
- ✓ A couple of curry leaves
- ✓ 1 tablespoon Asafetida powder
- ✓ Four chopped green chile peppers
- ✓ 1 cabbage head, finely sliced
- ✓ 14-cup frozen peas

Following Steps

1) Heat the oil in a large skillet over medium-high heat; in the heated oil, sauté the red chili peppers, all of the above-mentioned grains, and mustard. When the gram begins to brown, add the curry leaves and asafetida powder. Stir it thoroughly.

2) After adding the green chili peppers, cook for another 3 minutes.

3) Stir in the cabbage, peas, and lentils, season with salt, and cook for about 10 minutes, or until it begins to wilt but remains slightly crisp.

4) Cook for another 2 minutes after adding the coconut.

5) Serve immediately and enjoy.

Indian Dhal with Spinach

4 people can be served.

Time to cook: 2 hours.

- ✓ 2 cup yellow split peas (roughly 14 ounces)

- ✓ 8.4 quarts of water

- ✓ 2 tablespoons of freshly squeezed lemon juice (from one medium lemon)

- ✓ 2 teaspoons of kosher salt, plus more as needed.

- ✓ 8 teaspoons of unsalted butter (1 stick)

- ✓ 2 teaspoons cumin seeds

- ✓ 12 teaspoon turmeric powder

- ✓ 5 large garlic cloves, peeled and finely chopped.

- ✓ 14 cup fresh ginger, peeled and coarsely chopped

- ✓ 1 medium serrano chile, seeded and thinly sliced

- ✓ 8 ounces of cleaned and roughly chopped spinach.

Following Steps

Place the split peas in a fine-mesh strainer and quickly rinse them under cold water. Switch to a large pot, add the weighed water, and bring it to a boil over high heat.

2) Reduce the heat to medium-low and simmer for about 30 minutes, stirring occasionally and scraping any scum off the surface with a large spoon, or until the peas are completely soft and the split pea soup thickens.

3) Remove from the heat and stir in the lemon juice and salt to taste.

4) In a frying pan over medium heat, melt the butter until it foams.

Stir in the cumin seeds and turmeric and cook for about 3 minutes, or until the cumin seeds are roasted and aromatic and the butter is extremely frothy.

5) Stir in the garlic, ginger, and serrano, season with salt, and cook for 2 to 3 minutes, until the vegetables are softened, turning occasionally.Add the spinach and cook for about 4 minutes, turning occasionally, until the spinach has fully wilted.

Using the split peas, transfer the spinach mixture to the reserved pot and stir to combine. Serve with steamed rice or naan.

Masoor Daal

serves 4 people.

Time to cook: 2 hours.

ingredients

- ✓ 2 cups of sorted and drained dried masoor dal (called red lentils)
- ✓ 8.4 quarts of water
- ✓ 1 teaspoon of oil (flavored coconut oil or neutral)

- ✓ 1 large, coarsely diced yellow onion
- ✓ 6 minced garlic cloves.
- ✓ 1 teaspoon ginger, minced
- ✓ Two minced green chilies.
- ✓ 1 tablespoon of curry powder (Indian)
- ✓ 1 teaspoon whole mustard seeds
- ✓ 1 tablespoon coriander (cilantro)
- ✓ 12 tablespoon cumin
- ✓ 112 tsp salt (or to taste)
- ✓ 12 cups of fresh chopped tomatoes

Following Steps

Combine the lentils and water in a large container. Bring it to a boil, then reduce the pressure to a simmer. Cook it, partially covered with a lid, for about 15-20 minutes, or until the lentils are tender.

3) While the lentils are cooking, make the tadka. Warm a skillet over medium heat with a pinch of salt, oil, onion,

garlic, ginger, and chilies. Fry for about 5 minutes, or until the meat is cooked.

3) Stir in the spices, salt, curry powder, mustard, coriander, and cumin. Remove for 60 seconds to mix and prepare before adding the tomatoes. If using frozen tomatoes, cook for about 7 minutes, or until soft and saucy.

4) To season, add the tadka to the cooked lentils and cook for 5 minutes on low heat.

5) Serve with basmati rice and garnished with cilantro.And then there's serving.

Conclusion

With all of its unique items, strange sauces, and tongue-tingling flavors, Indian food can be both exciting and intimidating. It's a whole world of flavor.

To create a tantalizing culinary experience, you combine different techniques from other cuisines and include exotic spices. Do not be scared to experiment with Indian cuisine at home. To begin with, it is critical to consider the various foods and flavors that comprise Indian cuisine. Food in India is as popular as it is in Europe. All are completely novel, and the only thing they have in common is a judicious use of spices.

Cumin, coriander, turmeric, and ginger, to name a few, are key spices used in many recipes, and there are different ways to employ them. Spices have cardiovascular benefits as well as making a meal more tasty and interesting.

India's food is diverse in terms of history, geography, and environment. Spices are an important aspect of food preparation and are used to enhance the flavor of a dish. The correct use and combination of aromatic spices is crucial for the appropriate preparation of Indian food. Also, whether it's mustard oil in the north or coconut oil in the south, oil is a vital component in cooking. Vegetables vary depending on the season and region. The vegetables are prepared as a main course.

Vegetarians can benefit from Indian cuisine. For them, it is one of the most comfortable meals available. Seasonings and sauces are used sparingly to bring out the flavors of potatoes, cauliflower, spinach, and eggplant.

As you begin, keep things simple at home.

CPSIA information can be obtained
at www.ICGtesting.com
Printed in the USA
LVHW081944110222
710959LV00003B/23

9 783986 532291